AMERICAN
FOREIGN AID
DOCTRINES

By Edward C. Banfield

January, 1963

PUBLISHED AND DISTRIBUTED BY THE

AMERICAN ENTERPRISE INSTITUTE
FOR PUBLIC POLICY RESEARCH
WASHINGTON, D. C. 20036

AMERICAN ENTERPRISE INSTITUTE
For Public Policy Research

THE AMERICAN ENTERPRISE INSTITUTE FOR PUBLIC POLICY RESEARCH, established in 1943, is a nonpartisan research and educational organization which studies national policy problems.

Institute publications take two major forms:

1. LEGISLATIVE AND SPECIAL ANALYSES—factual analyses of current legislative proposals and other public policy issues before the Congress prepared with the help of recognized experts in the academic world and in the fields of law and government. A typical analysis features: (1) pertinent background, (2) a digest of significant elements, and (3) a discussion, pro and con, of the issues. The reports reflect no policy position in favor of or against specific proposals.

2. LONG-RANGE STUDIES—basic studies of major national problems of significance for public policy. The Institute, with the counsel of its Advisory Board, utilizes the services of competent scholars, but the opinions expressed are those of the authors and represent no policy position on the part of the Institute.

Contents

AMERICAN FOREIGN AID DOCTRINES[1]

... it is folly in one nation to look for disinterested favors from another; ... it must pay with a portion of its independence for whatever it may accept under that character; ... by such acceptance it may place itself in the condition of having given equivalents for nominal favors, and yet of being reproached with ingratitude for not giving more. There can be no greater error than to expect or calculate upon real favors from nation to nation. It is an illusion which experience must cure, which a just pride ought to discard.

Washington's Farewell Address

INTRODUCTORY

TECHNICAL ASSISTANCE and capital grants and loans to under-developed countries for non-military purposes ("foreign aid" or "aid") have in the last decade become a conspicuous feature of our foreign policy. In comparison with the total of defense spending the amount of aid has not been large (roughly 3 percent for the decade), and in comparison with gross national product it has been very small (less than 1 percent). But aid is nevertheless coming to be regarded as a principal instrument of our foreign policy. The use of it to supplement, and in some degree to substitute for, the traditional means of diplomacy is to be explained in part by the impracticability of using force or threats of force under the conditions that now prevail. Many people, however, believe it is in general a better way of achieving our objectives. In their widely read and

---

[1] This is a revision of a paper which appeared in *Public Policy*, C. J. Friedrich and S. E. Harris, eds. (Cambridge, Mass.: 1961). I am indebted to the Graduate School of Public Administration of Harvard University for permission to reprint from it.

The criticisms and suggestions of Professors Milton Friedman and Hans J. Morgenthau of the University of Chicago, of Professors Carl Kaysen, Martin Meyerson, Thomas C. Schelling, and Raymond Vernon of Harvard University, and of Mr. Joseph S. Nye, also of Harvard University, were particularly helpful.

influential book, Millikan and Rostow, for example, say that "we have put relatively too much emphasis in recent years on pacts, treaties, negotiations and international diplomacy and too little on measures to promote the evolution of stable, effective, and democratic societies abroad," and they emphasize this by subtitling their book "Key to an Effective Foreign Policy." [2]

In view of this great and increasing importance, it is surprising that the rationale of aid has not been better worked out. Many aspects of the subject have been analyzed in a penetrating way by serious writers, to be sure; economists and others have made valuable contributions in technical articles and books and, especially, in behind-the-scenes advice to administrators and policymakers. Few serious writers have dealt comprehensively with the theory of aid, however, and none of the serious writing seems to have entered significantly into "enlightened" public discussion of aid.[3] The terms of such discussion have been set almost entirely by publicists. The doctrines put forward by the publicists, although expressed in confident, hortatory tones as if they were well-established truths, consist mainly of unverified, and often unverifiable, assertions.

The present study examines critically the premises of these doctrines as to both fact and value. This examination, which involves reference to literature in economics, sociology, and political science, leads to the conclusion that there is at least as much to be said against aid as in favor of it. The question therefore arises: why is

---

[2] Max F. Millikan and W. W. Rostow, *A Proposal,* (New York: 1957), p. 4.

[3] A conspicuous exception is a paper by Thomas C. Schelling which was published by The American Assembly, Graduate School of Business, Columbia University, in *International Stability and Progress* (New York: June 1957); see also George Liska, *The New Statecraft* (Chicago: 1960); and Charles Wolf, Jr., *Foreign Aid: Theory and Practice in Southern Asia* (Princeton: 1960). A valuable collection of essays on foreign aid doctrines is soon to be published under the editorship of Robert A. Goldwin, director, Public Affairs Conference Center, University of Chicago, by Rand McNally and Co., Chicago. Among these essays is one by Max F. Millikan replying to some of the arguments of the present writer.

aid so confidently proposed by policymakers and so readily supported, or at any rate tolerated, by the public? This question requires consideration of the nature of American political culture and of democracy in general.

It should be noted that *doctrines* are under discussion here, not programs or practices. Foreign aid programs and practices may, of course, be very different from what the doctrines attempt to justify. It should be noted too that only *non-military* aid is under discussion.

The study is organized in three main parts. The first discusses the doctrines which justify non-military aid mainly or ultimately on the ground of its contribution to our national security. The second discusses the doctrines that justify it on other grounds. The third appraises the character of the discussion of aid doctrines and tries to show why the nature of American democracy has led to a sentimental and unworkable approach to the subject.

DOCTRINES JUSTIFYING AID BY NATIONAL SECURITY

MOST OF THOSE WHO write about aid justify it mainly or ultimately, but usually not solely, on the ground that it will contribute to national security. This position is based on one or the other of two largely incompatible doctrines.[1] One, which will be called the doctrine of indirect influence, asserts that national security will be promoted by using aid to transform fundamentally the cultures and institutions of the recipient countries. The other, which will be called the doctrine of direct influence, takes the cultures and institutions of the recipient countries as given and seeks to achieve the purpose (promotion of national security) by bringing influence to bear directly either upon the governments of the countries concerned or upon their public opinions.

The Doctrine of Indirect Influence

A widely accepted doctrine asserts that foreign aid may serve the vital interests of the United States by setting off, or bringing about, fundamental changes in the outlook and institutions of the recipient societies and that these changes will lead to others—especially the spread of freedom and democracy—that will promote peace and thus, indirectly, serve our ultimate purpose, which is to increase our national security.

Those who advocate the doctrine of indirect influence differ about how this process will work, especially about the nature of the changes to be produced by aid and how these will yield the further effects (freedom, democracy, and peace) that are desired ultimately. One school of thought emphasizes economic effects. A marked rise

---

[1] The two doctrines are largely incompatible in three ways: (1) the rightness of one depends logically to some extent upon the wrongness of the other (e.g., if transforming the recipient society is necessary, then a method which does not transform it is wrong; similarly, if transforming it is not necessary, there is no justification for a method which transforms it); (2) the two approaches compete for money, time, and other scarce resources; and (3) the success of one approach may entail, or even constitute, the non-success of the other (e.g., the transformation of a society may render the society unamenable to direct influence).

4

in average income will change profoundly the outlook of the masses of the people in underdeveloped countries. People who have enough to eat and something to look forward to will be much less receptive to Communist and other extremist appeals. Prosperity and opportunity will engender a taste for democracy and peace as, presumably, they have in own our society. The one great need, therefore, is to bring about rapid economic development. All the other effects that are desired will follow automatically.

On this theory, aid should be distributed among countries solely on the basis of their ability to use it to increase incomes. In principle, Russia and China might be given the highest priorities.

Another school of thought, represented principally by Millikan and Rostow, says that increases in income will not of themselves produce the desired effects (freedom, stability, democracy, and peace). To be sure, "some" economic improvement is a necessary condition for achieving these effects. But Millikan and Rostow are severely critical of the "crude materialist" thesis that economic development will of itself either reduce revolutionary pressures or lead to orderly political development. They regard it as a serious misconception to think that the spirit of revolt spreads easily among people who are chronically destitute or that the mere creation of wealth can satisfy a people's expectations. In their view, aid is important principally because it will set off social, political, and psychological changes which will energize the society.

> Even more important (than increases in income) are the confidence generated by the sense of progress, the social mobility, the outlet for leadership energies, the national unity, the consolidation of new individual and group values, and discovery of new sources of satisfaction and achievement which a concentration of social and economic development can bring.[2]

---

[2] Millikan and Rostow, *op. cit.*, pp. 25-26. Another version of the Millikan-Rostow doctrine appears in Senate Document 52, 85th Congress, 1st Session, July 1957, "The Objectives of United States Economic Assistance Programs" by the Center for International Studies, Massachusetts Institute of Technology. A reformulation of the M.I.T. position has recently been published: Max F. Millikan and Donald L. M. Blackmer, *The Emerging Nations: Their Growth and United States Policy* (Boston: 1961).

Since they insist that the desired effects can only be secured through certain social, political, and psychological changes, Millikan and Rostow might be expected to make suggestions for using aid to bring about these changes. They do not. All of their recommendations would be congenial to a "crude materialist." Whereas their first four chapters stress the crucial importance of non-economic factors, the remaining five chapters do not mention them. These later chapters refer to the purpose of aid as "economic development" and make recommendations that are all directed toward purely economic goals and that have little or no relation to (indeed, are probably somewhat in conflict with) the goal of setting off social, political, and psychological changes.[3] For example, the key recommendation is that the distribution of aid "be determined by absorptive capacity rather than by considerations of equity or politics."

Millikan and Rostow, then, not only say nothing about how the changes they regard as crucial are to be brought about, but, by laying out a program which looks entirely to economic objectives, they implicitly contradict the main point of their analysis.

Aid May Not Raise Levels of Living

All who hold the doctrine of indirect influence agree that a significant (Millikan and Rostow say "some") improvement in levels of living is necessary to secure the effects that are ultimately desired. "Crude materialists" believe that the greater the improvement the more marked these secondary effects will be. To the

---

[3] "We have a very specific purpose in adopting such a program: to promote the economic growth of the underdeveloped countries. . . ." (p. 64). The criteria listed in Chapter 7 all assume the purely economic goal. The recent reformulation of the M.I.T. doctrine (Millikan and Blackmer, *op. cit.*) is less subject to this criticism: it makes (Ch. 10) a number of suggestions for bringing about the necessary social, political, and psychological changes. But here also the greatest importance is given to purely economic criteria. For example, "Those responsible for development aid allocations must base their decisions on economic criteria rather than on considerations of short-run political advantage. In the long run our programs will be more likely to have the political consequences we seek if they are based on reasonably strict economic criteria." *Ibid.*, p. 120.

extent that there is reason to believe improvements will not take place, confidence in these doctrines must be weakened.

The improvement that is necessary is in the income of the ordinary man, not in aggregate income. A large increase in aggregate income could leave most people in the society worse off than before if, for example, population grew faster than income or if the growth in income was accompanied by an increased concentration of income in the hands of a small elite or was siphoned off for military or other governmental purposes that did not raise standards of life. In order to bring about the necessary improvement in levels of living, therefore, a proper equilibrium must be achieved among three variables: the productivity of the economy, the size of the population, and the evenness with which income is distributed. Conceivably a satisfactory relationship among these variables might be secured by changing only one of them; in the usual case, however, it will be essential to change them all.

In most of the underdeveloped areas aggregate income has been increasing in recent decades. These gains, however, are being nearly offset, and in some cases more than offset, by growth of population. The rate of population growth is in most places enough to absorb the increase in aggregate income that will result from normal saving. Although their incomes are rising, the underdeveloped countries, with some exceptions, are not increasing their per capita food supply.[4]

---

[4] See A. J. Jaffe, "Population Trends and Controls in Underdeveloped Countries," *Law and Contemporary Problems,* Vol. XXV:3, 1960, p. 528. According to J. J. Spengler, "Getting a fertility-reducing process under way today probably presupposes a saving rate of something like 10-15 percent of a nation's net national product . . . and the conversion of a sufficient fraction of it into forms of capital which are strongly production-oriented." "The Population Problem: Yesterday, Today, Tomorrow," *Southern Economic Journal,* Vol. XXVIII:3, 1961, p. 206. See also Kingsley Davis, "The Political Impact of New Population Trends," *Foreign Affairs,* Vol. 36:2, 1958, p. 296. Raymond Vernon believes steady improvement in the quality of censuses in the underdeveloped countries has led demographers to overestimate the rate of population growth and that per capita incomes are increasing faster than is usually thought (personal communication).

Estimates by Professor P. N. Rosenstein-Rodan on very optimistic assumptions (e.g., that the underdeveloped countries will get all the aid they can absorb and that they will make reasonably good use of it) indicate that from 1961 to 1976 gross national product in the underdeveloped parts of the world may rise from an average of $140 to $192 per capita.[5] Whether an increase of this magnitude would suffice to change the political outlook of the underdeveloped countries decidedly is, of course, anyone's guess. (It must be kept in mind that an increase in average income does not imply a better distribution of income; this may be such that most people will be no better off—conceivably even worse off—than at present. It should be taken into account, too, that the aspirations of the people of the underdeveloped parts of the world may meanwhile rise even faster than their incomes.)

If the aid doctrine requires not merely *some* improvement in levels of living but the "modernization" of the economy, the outlook is even more discouraging. That aggregate and in some cases per capita incomes in these countries have been growing in recent years does not mean that they will continue to do so. The growth that has occurred so far may be in the nature of "taking up slack"; additional growth may be impossible without basic changes within the societies —changes that will not occur.

Some societies may never develop. The American Indian is a case in point. The cruelty, indifference, and stupidity of whites can explain only in part why many Indian cultures have not entered modern society after several hundred years of contact with it. In the last 30 years a vast amount of effort has been put forth on behalf of the Indians. The United States Government, for example, has spent several thousand dollars per Navaho to help them adapt, and has spent it with much intelligence and good will—as much, at any

---

[5] See Millikan and Blackmer, *op. cit.*, p. 154. A. J. Jaffe's conclusion, in the article cited above, was that "Under the best of circumstances, it will still take at least one generation, counting from the end of World War II, before there may be a decided slackening in the rate of population growth and a very significant improvement in the levels of living." (p. 534).

rate, as is likely to be found in any underdeveloped country. Yet the problem of the Navaho remains almost as it was a generation ago.[6]

Even those underdeveloped countries which are not primitive may lack certain cultural or other prerequisites of development. One such prerequisite is the presence in the society of at least a small class of persons having talents and incentives that lead them to organize, innovate, and take risks. Other prerequisites are traits which must probably be fairly widespread in order for such a class to arise, or to function effectively if it does arise. These include the desire for material improvement,[7] the belief that economic activity is worthy of respect,[8] willingness to concert activity for common purposes or at least to allow others to concert it without interference[9] and ability

---

[6] See Frank A. Tinker, "The Navaho Experience," *Challenge,* December 1960, pp. 26-30.

[7] Capital formation, Nurkse says, can be permanently successful only in a capital-conscious community. "Nothing matters so much as the quality of the people." Initiative, prudence, ingenuity, and foresightedness are the qualities particularly needed. Ragnar Nurkse, *Problems of Capital Formation in Underdeveloped Countries* (Oxford: 1953), p. 155. Professor Edward S. Mason has remarked that it is not clear that the people of southern Asia are uniformly and significantly motivated by a desire for economic betterment. *Promoting Economic Development* (Claremont, California: 1955), p. 41.

[8] In the newly developing states, according to Edward A. Shils, the nation is the sole locus of charisma; political leaders get their legitimacy from it. For development to occur, some ambition must be turned into economizing behavior and this can only happen as such behavior is seen as permeated by the sacred. In most underdeveloped areas there is no such tradition; "It cannot of course be created deliberately," Shils says, "but it can be helped to grow by the establishment of favorable conditions. Successful enterprise will help to create it, but so will a sympathetic and appreciative public opinion in the underdeveloped countries." Edward A. Shils, "The Concentration and Dispersal of Charisma," *World Politics,* Vol. XI:1, 1958, p. 18.

[9] See E. C. Banfield, *The Moral Basis of a Backward Society* (Glencoe: 1958).

to maintain at least that minimum of political stability that is essential in order for the Government to carry out certain critical tasks.

These and other prerequisites are not all present in any of the underdeveloped areas.[10]

Such factors are in general more important obstacles to development than are lack of technical knowledge or of foreign capital. If cultural and other conditions favor development, it will occur without aid. (Japan and Russia, to cite recent cases, did in fact develop without it.) If cultural conditions do not favor development, no amount of aid will bring it about. (Cuba and Haiti, for example, have received large amounts of both technical assistance and foreign capital without development taking place.) Probably no country is so poor that it cannot accumulate capital,[11] and the Western world could not if it tried prevent the wholesale borrowing of its technical knowledge by underdeveloped countries able to make use of it. Where populations have a "will" to limit births, the population

----

[10] After listing four prerequisites of development "each as critical as capital" (viz., a substantial degree of literacy and that small number of people with knowledge and skills for managerial and technical tasks, a substantial measure of social justice, a reliable apparatus of government and public administration, and a clear and purposeful view of what development involves), J. K. Galbraith declares that "In practice, one or more of these four factors is missing in most of the poor countries." "A Positive Approach to Foreign Aid," *Foreign Affairs*, Vol. 39:3, 1961, pp. 444-57. Professor Simon Kuznets has observed that it is not the physical equipment of a country that constitutes the major part of its capital but rather "the body of knowledge amassed from tested findings and the capacity and training of the population to use this knowledge effectively." In United Nations, *Processes and Problems of Industrialization in Under Developed Countries* (New York: 1955), p. 5. See also T. W. Schultz, "Investment in Human Capital," *American Economic Review* Vol. LI:1, 1961, pp. 1-17. For discussions of the cultural conditions of growth, see Ralph Braibanti and J. J. Spengler, *Traditions, Values, and Socio-Economic Development* (Durham, N. C.: 1961).

[11] Cf. Simon Kuznets, *Six Lectures on Economic Growth* (Glencoe: 1959), pp. 80-81.

10

problem will solve itself; where they do not, there is nothing much that can be done.[12]

But even if all cultural and institutional prerequisites of growth were present, it might not be possible for certain underdeveloped countries ever to achieve levels of living even roughly approximating those of the West. A modern economy must draw upon a large complex of basic raw materials, including land, water, fossil fuels, and minerals of many kinds. Even with free international trade, shortages of some resource would set limits on the level of development that some of the most disadvantaged countries—India, for example—could achieve.[13]

It should not be surprising if a donor over-values his gift. American aid doctrine certainly exaggerates greatly the importance of both technical assistance and foreign capital in the development process. Only in the most backward countries can either kind of aid make a crucial difference, or perhaps even an important one. In the nature of the case, the greater the need of a country for aid, the less evidence there is that it has a capability to develop. The most prosperous and promising of the underdeveloped countries—Mexico, for example—may not require any aid in order to grow at a satisfactory rate. There is, to be sure, an important middle group of countries— India is a conspicuous example—which can absorb large amounts of aid and which offer some promise of developing. In time, too, some of the most backward countries may be brought by aid to the condition of this middle group. Nevertheless, despite these qualifications, there is a built-in perversity in the situation which makes it impossible to use large amounts of aid with effectiveness in most places.

---

[12] The existence of a cheap and effective oral contraceptive does not put it within the power of governments to reduce population growth; a reduction will occur only as there is a widespread desire within the societies in question to limit births, and this will not arise except in consequence of general improvement in levels of living. See Robert C. Cook's article in the issue of *Law and Contemporary Problems* cited above, p. 387.

[13] See Richard L. Meier, *Science and Economic Development* (New York: 1956).

11

Although aid is seldom, or perhaps never, an indispensable prerequisite to economic development and although even under the most favorable circumstances it is not likely to be the "key" to development, it may, as both Milton Friedman and J. K. Galbraith have emphasized, do much to retard development if improperly used.[14] There is much that should be done by government in underdeveloped areas (e.g., provision of roads, elementary education, a monetary system, law and order), Friedman says, but there are crucial advantages in letting private business do as much as possible. One such advantage is that private individuals, since they risk their own funds, have a much stronger incentive to invest wisely. Another is that private individuals are more likely than state bureaucracies to abandon unsuccessful ventures. The availability of resources at little or no cost to a country inevitably stimulates "monument-building," i.e., investment in projects adding little or nothing to the productivity of the economy. Under these circumstances, he concludes, countries would develop faster without aid than with it.

Even if it does begin, economic development may not last very long or get very far. Continued growth, David McCord Wright has pointed out, involves discovery and use of new ideas.[15] The developing society must produce a social outlook, institutions, and economic organization which, generation after generation, will bring to the fore men who will produce new ideas. That such men come to the fore in one generation, Wright observes, is no guarantee that they will in the next. The long-run economic prospect, therefore, is very uncertain in any society, including, of course, a highly developed one like our own.

---

[14] There is a striking agreement between Friedman and Galbraith with respect to most of these points. See Milton Friedman, "Foreign Economic Aid: Means and Objectives," *The Yale Review*, Summer 1958, and J. K. Galbraith, *Economic Development in Perspective* (Cambridge: 1962).

[15] David McCord Wright, "Stages of Growth vs. The Growth of Freedom," *Fortune*, December 1959.

The Political Prospects

But even if economic growth does occur it will not necessarily lead to the spread of freedom and democracy. In the literature on aid these terms are usually left undefined. One cannot tell which is meant: wide distribution of power, rule of law, regard for civil liberties, free elections, consumers' choice, national independence, a distribution system favoring the poor, or something else. Obviously these need not all go together (e.g., national independence is compatible with dictatorship). Obviously measures that promote democracy or freedom in one meaning may inhibit them in others.

If by democracy and freedom are meant "respect for the individual" and its corollary "government by discussion" (however these principles are expressed institutionally), there is certainly little basis for optimism. Respect for the individual is unique to the Judaeo-Christian tradition. In those parts of the world which do not participate in this tradition, the idea is unintelligible or nearly so. That a conception so fundamental might enter into and transform alien cultures would be highly improbable under the most favorable of circumstances. That this particular conception—of the sacredness of the individual—might enter into and transform alien cultures in those parts of the world where the worthlessness of the individual human life is a conspicuous fact of everyday experience (a circumstance which indeed constitutes the very problem that aid seeks to solve) is so improbable as to be incredible.

The prospects are better if democracy is defined to mean merely government through institutions that are in some sense representative (i.e., which take account of the wants and interests of the major elements of the population and which by a peaceful process like an election can be made to respond to public opinion). But democracy even in this restricted sense will have a slow and fitful growth in most of the underdeveloped world. The political institutions of the West cannot be copied, as its technology can, by people whose ways of thinking and valuing are fundamentally different. It took several hundred years for the West to arrive at its very imperfect democracy.

13

The underdeveloped countries, although they may learn something from our experience, are not likely to do much better.[16]

The possibilities for development of societies that share our most fundamental ethical premises are probably best in Latin America, which has participated in Western civilization for four and one-half centuries. But even there the long-run outlook for democracy is very uncertain.

Even if mere "political stability" (i.e., the absence of change brought about by violence) is taken as the goal, the prospect is not good. Economic development, by hastening the decay of tradition and other forms of authority, will create ferment and disorder. The spread of literacy, an indispensable condition of self-sustaining growth, is especially likely to do so. As Millikan and Rostow say:

> The education which accompanies economic change contributes to unrest. People who can't read can't be subverted by literature. Once they can read, the process of widening knowledge and changing ideas of what the world is like and what is possible in it proceeds with great rapidity.[17]

Urbanization, another indispensable condition of growth, also tends to produce political instability. According to Bert F. Hoselitz:

> . . . the greater degree of literacy and the much greater degree of exposure to mass communication media make urban populations more susceptible to various forms of political propaganda. Thus, at present, the cities of underdeveloped countries, and above all their primate cities, are the centers of nationalist sentiment and political

---

[16] Seymour Martin Lipset concludes a valuable analysis of some of these questions with a quotation from Max Weber: "The spread of Western cultural and capitalist economy did not, *ipso facto*, guarantee that Russia would also acquire the liberties which had accompanied their emergence in European history . . . European liberty had been born in unique, perhaps unrepeatable, circumstances at a time when the intellectual and material conditions for it were exceptionally propitious." Lipset believes that, despite this dim outlook, encouraging the spread of democracy "remains perhaps the most important substantive intellectual task which students of politics can still set before themselves." "Some Social Requisites of Democracy: Economic Development and Political Legitimacy," *American Political Science Review*, Vol. LIII:1, 1959, p. 103.

[17] *Op. cit.*, p. 22.

14

action. But to the extent that aspirations for economic advancement are not fulfilled or fulfilled only inadequately, urban populations may become a very responsible element for radical propaganda of various sorts and may easily be induced to support forms of totalitarian policies on the left or on the right.[18]

In India, Asia, Africa, and Latin America the more economically developed regions have been more prone to violence than the less developed ones.[19]

If aid raises the level of expectation in a country without affording a steady accompanying increase in actual satisfaction, it is, perhaps, more likely than not to create discontent and revolution. This is the implication of an analysis by James C. Davies. According to him:

> Revolutions are most likely to occur when a prolonged period of objective economic and social development is followed by a short period of sharp reversal. The all-important effect on the minds of people in a particular society is to produce, during the former period, an expectation of continued ability to satisfy needs—which continue to rise—and, during the latter, a mental state of anxiety and frustration when manifest reality breaks away from anticipated reality. The actual state of socio-economic development is less significant than the expectation that past progress, now blocked, can and must continue in the future.[20]

In most parts of the underdeveloped world the real question is not whether there can be created a political system that is democratic or stable, but whether there can be created one capable of modernizing the country at all. "No new state,'" Edward A. Shils has written, "can modernize itself and remain or become liberal and democratic without an elite of force of character, intelligence and high moral qualities." Very few of the underdeveloped countries, he says, have such elites; those that do have them may under favorable circumstances enjoy democracy that is to some extent tutelary,

[18] Bert F. Hoselitz, *Sociological Aspects of Economic Growth* (Glencoe: 1960), pp. 228-29.

[19] For an illuminating discussion of these matters with respect to India, see Bert F. Hoselitz and Myron Weiner, "Economic Development and Political Stability," *Dissent*, Spring 1961.

[20] James C. Davies, "Toward a Theory of Revolution," *American Sociological Review*, 27:1 (February 1962), p. 6.

and in time, if the elite has a very powerful will to be democratic, the enormous gap between it and the masses of the population may be overcome. The less democratic and much more probable alternatives will not, he thinks, provide stable government at all:

> The alternatives are disorderly oligarchies, each promising and aspiring to maintain order and to modernize, but doing so only by sweeping the disorder temporarily into a box from which it recurrently springs out into full strength. The totalitarian oligarchy by the ruthlessness of its elite and by the vigor of its party machine as well as by the organizational and material aid which it would get from the Soviet Union, would appear to have the best chance to maintain itself, once it gets into power. But it too would have to compromise markedly with the human materials which traditional society gives it. It could build monuments and suppress open dissatisfaction but it could not realize its idea.[21]

The expansion of state activity which aid engenders tends in some ways to discourage the growth of democracy. In a prosperous and politically experienced society, democracy and extensive governmental participation in economic affairs may coexist. But the situation of the underdeveloped countries precludes this. The best choice open to many of them is between governments that are not incompetent and ones that are not tyrannical; the possibility of having

---

[21] Shils describes "components" and "preconditions" of five possible courses of political development in the new states: A. Political democracy ("*civilian rule* through *representative institutions* in the matrix of *public liberties*"); B. Tutelary democracy (political democracy adapted to provide a greater preponderance of the executive); C. Modernizing oligarchies (civilian or military cliques reduce parliament to a ratifying role, depend upon the civil service, and do not tolerate an independent judiciary); D. Totalitarian oligarchy (oligarchy with democratic airs and a doctrine); E. Traditional oligarchy (a firm dynastic constitution, buttressed by traditional religious beliefs). With respect to each of these, he discusses the following preconditions: a. the stability, coherence, and effectiveness of the ruling elite, b. the practice and acceptance of opposition, c. the machinery of authority, d. the institutions of public opinion, and e. the civil order. See his two articles on "Political Development in the New States," *Comparative Studies in Society and History*, Vol. II (1960). The quotations are from the second article, pp. 407 and 410.

governments that are *neither* incompetent *nor* tyrannical does not exist. Aid, by encouraging governments to undertake tasks beyond their capabilities, is likely to lead to waste through the incompetence of the recipients, to the extension and hardening of governmental power—or, perhaps most likely, to both at once.[22]

Development at what is now in the underdeveloped areas considered to be a reasonable rate will require much more saving than is likely to occur voluntarily. Governments can secure some of the needed saving by defrauding their populations through inflation, the use of government marketing boards, and other devices. To the extent that fraud does not suffice, they are likely to use force; as the required amount of savings increases (i.e., as the desired rate of development increases), the amount of repression will probably also increase. According to Sir Robert Jackson:

> Heroic measures of internal saving (and 15 percent of national income *is* heroic when consumption is marginal and population growing by 2 per cent a year) demand a ruthless political discipline which liberal systems can hardly employ and still remain liberal. Totalitarian dictatorship can thus appear not simply the short cut but the only route to economic growth.[23]

---

[22] "Perhaps the greatest unsolved problem of the Indians is to find some way to insure efficient public entrepreneurship under the general aegis of a parliamentary government." J. K. Galbraith, "Rival Economic Theories in India," *Foreign Affairs*, July 1958, p. 596. "Under the general aegis" may perhaps be interpreted to mean "under the nominal control of." E. S. Mason, *op. cit.*, p. 49, writes: "The magnitude of the role assumed by the state in promoting economic development raises the question of whether the governments of southern Asia are up to the job."

[23] Sir Robert G. A. Jackson, *The Case for an International Development Authority* (Syracuse: 1959), p. 40. Egypt is a case in point.

"Unless it is resigned to a continuance of the decline of the living standards of the masses, the government of Egypt must find the means for sharply increasing the accumulation of capital and directing it into productive channels. This is likely to require deficit financing and a program of forced savings. In other words, Egypt must curtail present levels of consumptions, or even depress them, in order to achieve even a modest rate of economic development." Frederick Harbison and Ibrahim Abdelkader Ibrahim, *Human Resources for Egyptian Enterprise* (New York: 1958), p. 34.

17

Some underdeveloped countries may have to adopt totalitarian methods in order to meet the threat presented by neighboring countries which have adopted them and are developing faster than they.[24]

The exigencies of development, then, will tend to bring into existence repressive or totalitarian regimes. But even without these exigencies, the same effect might arise from other causes. The rulers of the underdeveloped countries are discovering that the technology of mass communications affords them the possibility of rule by propaganda. This is something new in the history of the world. In very poor societies it was formerly uneconomic, if not altogether impossible, to maintain rule by force over a large area. Consequently government was mostly village or tribal and rested largely on traditional authority. The situation has now changed fundamentally. The technology of communications makes it feasible to govern by talk rather than by force, and to do so over an almost limitless area at a cost that is trivial even by the standards of a poor society.[25] Even if rulers did not need to increase their power in order to hasten

---

[24] Barbara Ward Jackson finds that the Congress Party of India is well suited for the give-and-take of democracy. "But it is not a very suitable instrument for rallying vast unified popular effort or for exacting great public sacrifice. It follows that India cannot mobilize savings and direct energies as the Chinese Communists claim to do, and Congress as a political party can survive only so long as really heroic sacrifices are not needed from the Indian people." "India on the Eve of its Third Plan," *Foreign Affairs,* January 1961, p. 265.

[25] The following dispatch was carried by Reuters, datelined Panama, May 6, 1961:

Portable transistor radios are becoming a key factor in Latin-American politics, according to leading radio and television executives in Panama.

Their role is to bring politicians' messages, appeals and, upon occasion, speeches to hundreds of thousands of peasants who never had any form of direct communication with the politically-active cities.

The core of the role played by these transistor radios in bringing about this change is the flashlight batteries on which so many of the sets operate.

The humblest country store stocks them for countryfolk who live far beyond the end of the last power line. A recent survey showed that one-third of the population of Latin America comes into this category.

economic development, they would probably find the opportunity for rule by propaganda irresistible.

Rule by propaganda requires a constant supply of program material, of ideas exciting or challenging enough to stir the masses into a state of mind that will make them amenable to control. "Positive" appeals for "constructive" action—appeals, say, for great national crusades against poverty, disease, and ignorance—may serve the purpose. In general, however, appeals to hate and fear will probably work better. The example of Castro suggests that excoriating the capitalist, the colonialist, the foreigner, the Yankee, and (although not in Cuba) the white man is likely to be the cheapest, easiest and most dependable way to rally the people, make them cohere as a nation, and secure possession of their energies and loyalties.

Where propaganda is to be the basis of governmental power, the West is at a great and probably hopeless disadvantage. It is identified (unfairly, of course, in the case of the United States) with the hated system of colonialism, the horrors of which increase with every retelling and the virtues of which have already been forgotten. The great principles for which the West stands, such as the worth of the individual, are unintelligible to the masses in the underdeveloped areas; the meaning of democracy, it need hardly be said, cannot be shouted over the radio to a street mob. The Communists, on the other hand, are under no such handicaps. The Marxist ideology is, as Adam B. Ulam has remarked, the *natural* one for backward societies to adopt.[26] It provides people who are undergoing transition from a pre-industrial to an industrial society with a doctrine that makes sense of what must otherwise appear to them a senseless world. The Soviet Union, moreover, is an underdeveloped country that has "made good," whereas the United States, the richest country by far, is the conspicuous symbol of all that is hateful and threatening.

---

[26] Adam B. Ulam, *The Unfinished Revolution* (New York: 1960), Ch. VII. See also Zbigniew Brzezinski, "The Politics of Underdevelopment," *World Politics,* Vol. IX:1, 1956, p. 63 and *passim,* and the contrasting views of Alex Inkeles, "The Soviet Union: Model for Asia?" *Problems of Communism,* Vol. VIII:6, 1959, pp. 30-38.

In some countries of Africa, the Middle East, and Latin America, leaders and followers alike are stirred less by desire for improvement of living standards than by the emotion of nationalism—by the desire to create a mystic bond among a chosen people marked by some sacred stigmata and to exalt the power and the glory of the nation. This is an expression of a primordial urge to be in contact with the sacred and to feel awe and reverence. Economic development, where nationalism is strongest, is valued less for itself (it may even be thought intrinsically undesirable) than as a means of symbolizing, or of asserting, the power and glory of the nation. To people intensely moved by the religion of nationalism, those who do not belong to the nation are beyond the pale: their mere presence defiles the sacred places. The existence of the nation as a mystic body depends upon maintaining this radical distinction between those within and those without.

These reasons for hating the West, the capitalist, the white, and the foreigner exist in some degree in most of the underdeveloped countries. They account in part for the hostility often manifested toward the United States by the leaders of countries which have no "objective" grounds for hostility. In such countries, it may be much more important to the ruling clique, and perhaps also to the whole nation, to have us for enemies than for friends.

Successful application of the doctrine of indirect influence (supposing this to be possible) will require concentration of aid efforts on the most promising and amenable countries, and this, of course, will almost certainly create disaffection among those that are not favored. It is quite likely that the promising and amenable—and hence favored—countries will be ones of little strategic importance to the United States and that the disfavored—and hence disaffected—ones will be of great strategic importance.[27]

---

[27] Chester Bowles, a special adviser to the President, proposed publicly on August 14, 1962 that the Agency for International Development classify applicants in four priority categories according to their ability and willingness to make use of aid. Bowles went so far as to list particular countries he thought might be included in the two top categories. He acknowledged that the exigencies of Cold War (or other) politics might require giving

Developed Societies Not Necessarily Peaceful

If the underdeveloped countries were to become fully developed and "modernized," they would not necessarily be peaceful. As Rupert Emerson has observed:

> The great wars which have seriously threatened mankind in recent history have taken place within the fraternity of the rich and developed states. Can there be any clear assurance of a gain for peace in the multiplication of well-to-do, industrialized states, modeled precisely after those which have been the principal warmakers of modern times?[28]

The disparity between the richness of some nations and the poverty of others does not, as is so often asserted, tend toward war. Poor, pre-industrial nations do not attack rich, industrial ones, much as they might like to. Nor does being "undemocratic" incline one nation to attack another if the attack cannot possibly be successful.

By the same token, any nation, however developed or democratic, may be aggressive. Millikan and Rostow have no basis for their confidence that democratic societies "can be relied upon not to generate conflict because their own national interests parallel ours and because they are politically healthy and mature."[29] On the contrary, it may be taken for granted that in the long course of history the interests of any nation are likely to conflict with those of any other, including, of course, the United States, and that when this happens the relative power of the nations, not their political "health" or "maturity," will determine the outcome.

Millikan and Rostow assert that as underdeveloped countries gain confidence they will become easier to deal with.

> Once they see that they are wholly capable of standing on their own feet, they can afford to be less quixotic and nervous in their foreign

---

aid to countries not qualifying by the "economic and social" criteria. These would be "exceptional cases," he said, and might be financed from the Special Contingency budget. The approach he recommended was "tough-minded," he said, and conservatives would "applaud and support" it.

[28] Rupert Emerson, *From Empire to Nation* (Cambridge: 1960), p. 415.
[29] *Op. cit.,* p. 4.

policies. A confident nation, making progress at home, is likely to conduct its foreign policy with poise and good sense.[30]

This also overlooks the fact of power. The Soviet Union is a confident nation, but it is nevertheless infinitely dangerous to us. Twenty-five years ago, when its confidence was much less, it was no danger at all. The difference is that its power has increased. What counts is not the confidence of nations but their power. The peace of the world would be perfectly safe if the underdeveloped nations (and the others also!) were utterly without confidence, providing they were also utterly without power.

Finally, if the countries in question were to become entirely peaceable, our national security would not necessarily be increased and it might even be decreased. It would not be increased if we possessed deterrents sufficient to prevent any nation, warlike or peaceable, from attacking us, and it might be decreased if countries now willing to risk war in support of our policy were (having become peaceable) no longer willing to do so.

The Probability of Success

The degree of confidence that one has in the doctrine of indirect influence will therefore depend upon how one judges four probabilities: (a) that aid will increase per capita incomes significantly, (b) that this increase, by itself or with other energizing changes, will make societies more democratic, (c) that their being more democratic will make them more peaceable, and (d) that their being more peaceable will add to our security. The probability of the outcome that is ultimately desired, viz., greater national security, is the *product* of these four separate probabilities. Hence (to assign numbers for illustrative purposes only) if there is one chance in ten that per capita incomes will increase significantly, one chance in ten that this will make the societies more democratic, one chance in ten that this will make them peaceable, and one chance in ten that their being peaceable will increase our security, there is one chance in

---

[30] *Ibid.,* p. 32.

ten thousand of achieving our ultimate aim in the manner the doctrine prescribes.

Along with the probability of achieving the effect that is ultimately desired must be considered another: that of achieving it *in time*. The peril to America exists now and in the immediate future; it makes little difference to us how peaceful the presently underdeveloped countries will be 100 years from now, or even 30 years from now, if by then we will have been destroyed. One unit of present advantage is worth much more to us than many units of advantage 30 years hence, and more, perhaps, than any possible number 100 years hence. It is certainly wildly optimistic to believe that the underdeveloped areas may become "mature" and "healthy" democracies within a generation, but even if they did, success might come too late.

The rate of technological and other change is so great that the present crisis of relations between the West and the Soviets is very likely to have been resolved one way or another in less than 30 years. If our objectives can be achieved simply by inspiring the underdeveloped countries to "confident" and "constructive" efforts—if, that is, we need not first raise their incomes substantially—this problem of timing is less urgent. But it is very hard to believe that our objectives *can* be achieved in this way.

Whatever the benefits that may be judged probable on this basis, account must also be taken of the costs. One cost which may not be obvious is the possibility of making matters worse. We may, for example, set off armaments races and wars between the underdeveloped countries. Indeed, there is reason to suppose that we have already done so. Israel's attack on Egypt was probably made possible by American aid, for, although the aid was non-military it freed foreign exchange for the purchase of armaments. In time, perhaps, our non-military aid to Egypt will enable that country to attack Israel. The arms competition between India and Pakistan is largely financed by us. By giving India non-military aid we make it possible for her to buy arms (Indian expenditures for arms have for several years equalled the value of the aid received from us) and this causes Pakistan to demand ever-larger amounts of military assistance. We are therefore financing both sides of an arms race.

This is not the only danger. We ourselves may eventually be menaced by countries that are now weak and friendly but will by our aid be made strong and hostile. It was American aid to nationalist China that gave the Chinese Communists their start. "It is one of the cheerful illusions of our day," Rupert Emerson has remarked, "that economic and social development will surely redound to the benefit of the West."[31]

What economists call "opportunity costs" must not be overlooked either. By following one course of action we are to some extent precluded from following others. The net benefits of actions foregone must be counted as costs against the actions that are taken. For example, if for fear of jeopardizing some long-run gain that is to be had by transforming the economic and political life of a recipient country we fail to take actions that would benefit us in the short run, the loss of the short-run benefits must be counted as a cost against the gain in the long-run benefits. To give another example, to the extent that aid for non-defense purposes interferes with, or precludes, measures for defense purposes, the loss in terms of the latter must be charged as a cost against the former.

The Doctrine of Direct Influence

Another doctrine asserts that aid may serve the vital interests of the United States by directly influencing the recipient governments and peoples to act as the interests of the United States require or, more often, to refrain from acting in ways injurious to the United States. In contrast to the doctrine of indirect influence, this doctrine does not expect aid to work by changing the character of the recipient society economically or otherwise, though it acknowledges that economic and other effects may be by-products.

Several versions of this doctrine may usefully be distinguished:

1. *Quid Pro Quo.* The aid is part of a bargain between two governments in which there are clearly specified advantages to both sides. For example, we might agree to build a system of highways

---

[31] *Op. cit.,* p. 411.

24

in return for assurances that the Soviet Union would not be allowed to penetrate the country.

Bribery is a special case. Here the bargain is with politicians in the underdeveloped country who act from personal interest rather than duty.

2. *Business Friendship.* The aid is given to create or maintain a relationship that is expected to have mutual advantages over time. The aid is, so to speak, a payment on an open account, it being tacitly understood that political advantages will be given in return.

3. *Maintenance of Friendly Governments.* The aid is intended to strengthen and to keep in power a government which is friendly, or at least not unfriendly. This may be done by undertakings, including of course economic development, which will increase the prestige of the recipient government or the confidence its public have in it.

4. *Prestige.* The aid is intended to exhibit dramatically the power of the giver and thereby to increase it. As Hobbes said in the *Leviathan,* "Reputation of power is power, because it draweth with it the adherence of those that need protection."

5. *Good Will.* The aid is intended to make the recipient feel well disposed toward the giver and to put him under an implied obligation to return kindness for kindness. Few people expect governments to be moved by such sentiments as gratitude, but it is fairly widely believed that public opinion may be so moved and that it may have some effect on the policy of governments.

6. *Moral Force.* The aid is expected to affect public opinion by exerting moral force. The giver expects that the nobility of his action will inspire the recipient to act nobly too.

In most discussions of the doctrine of direct influence, these differences of approach are not clearly recognized. The term "impact" is sometimes used to describe any approach that is expected to make its effect by influencing opinion. It is evident, however, that different approaches require different means. For example, measures to promote "business friendship" would not generate "moral force." Distinctions along these lines are therefore implied even when they are not made expressly.

Those who make any distinctions of this kind at all usually disdain the approaches at the "quid pro quo" end of the scale and approve those at the "moral force" end. David Lilienthal, for example, says that the policy of extending aid in order to buy the allegiance of the underdeveloped countries, or to keep the Soviets from buying it, has not worked, cannot be made to work and has got us into a "moral mess." He asks:

> What can we say in defense of an American policy, however disguised with diplomatic rhetoric, which from time to time displays the representatives of a noble nation up to their elbows in the cynical international bazaar, there to bargain and haggle and make deals by which we trade our money or credit or technical aid for "friendship."[32]

Lilienthal favors the moral force approach. He urges a program of aid from which we would seek nothing for ourselves and which would therefore give the world "a demonstration of the kind of people our system of political and economic freedom is capable of producing."

> We could [he says] provide an example by which the rapidly emerging nations of the world could weigh and judge the virtue of making increasing freedom for the individual—with justice for his neighbor—the cornerstone of their own evolving societies.

Hans J. Morgenthau, although he does not condemn the "quid pro quo" and "business friendship" approaches, also emphasizes "moral force":

> This plausibility of the American purpose, established in the eyes of the world by deeds, must again become the foundation upon which, supported by the modern techniques of propaganda and foreign aid, the world-wide influence of America must rest.[33]

It is worth noting that Morgenthau couples propaganda with aid and that he puts propaganda first. The objective of "impact" aid

---

[32] David Lilienthal, "Needed: A New Credo for Foreign Aid," *New York Times Magazine,* June 26, 1960. J. K. Galbraith says that our aid should be seen "as a manifestation of the quality of the society—as an index of its generosity and compassion and hence its right to respect." *The Liberal Hour* (New York: 1960), p. 22.

[33] Hans J. Morgenthau, *The Purpose of American Politics* (New York: 1960), p. 28.

is to create an opinion favorable to the United States, not to change the conditions of life in the underdeveloped country except as doing so may be necessary in order to create a favorable opinion. Though deeds, as Morgenthau says, are a necessary condition of effective propaganda, they count only as the accompanying propaganda makes them count; to the extent that this propaganda fails to turn them to account by changing opinion, they are wasted. It follows, then, that if "impact" can be increased by spending more on propaganda and less on deeds, we ought to make the change.

It is not obvious why Americans so generally condemn the "quid pro quo" and "business friendship" versions of the direct influence doctrine. To bribe a foreign statesman to keep his country free may not be evil at all. But if it is, it is a kind of evil that respectable statesmen have always deemed it their duty to do when the security and welfare of their countries demanded. Where bribery is not involved, the justification of "reason of state" is not necessary. If a government is willing to give political favors in exchange for material resources, it is hard to see why either it or a government which accepts its offer should be criticized. As Aristotle remarked, the expression "friendly governments" means governments that exchange favors, not ones that love each other.

The other ways of exercising influence are in fact open to moral objections that cannot be made against bargains. In a bargain, each party decides for itself whether it is willing to do as the other wants and, if so, on what terms. That is to say neither is manipulated by the other. The other modes of influence, including of course "moral force," *do* involve manipulation; they are exercised unilaterally, and if a party responds to influence, it does so without necessarily being aware that it is being manipulated: without, that is, realizing that the favor or generous deed was done simply to elicit the response wanted by the influencer.[34]

---

[34] Some countries are said to find the moral claims implied by gifts particularly odious. For this reason, apparently, the Soviets offer credits rather than grants. Their propaganda in the underdeveloped countries stresses the mutual benefit of aid arrangements rather than the generosity of the Soviets. Joseph S. Berliner, *Soviet Economic Aid* (New York: 1958), p. 147.

27

Instead of regretting the occasional necessity of putting aid on a business basis, we should wish that we could do it more often. Unfortunately our opportunities will be few. The underdeveloped countries are in most cases pathologically sensitive about national "honor," and the suggestion that we should get something for what we give is always bitterly resented. Only the most reactionary governments—those without ideology, which exist more or less as the private possession of a monarch or a ruling clique—will sell political favors. Doing business with these will make it all the harder to come to terms with the ideologically-based governments that will eventually replace them. Though the purchase of political favors may be indispensable as an expedient in some cases, it is not a widely available possibility.

For the United States to seek to increase its prestige by the use of aid makes little sense. The power of this country is not underrated. (The Soviets are in a different position; their power is new and has to be seen to be believed.) Military prestige, moreover, is of little value so long as it is understood on all sides that Soviet power, world opinion, and our own scruples will prevent us from using force in any event. Our experience with Cuba is a case in point. The case for using aid to increase our reputation for non-military power is even poorer. No underdeveloped country doubts our ability to give or withhold enormous advantages.

"Good will" and "moral force" can make their effect only by working upon public opinion rather than upon governments. The public opinion of an underdeveloped country does not include the opinion of the peasants, who in most places are the vast majority. If our grain prevents the peasant from starving, he may be grateful, but his gratitude has no effect upon the policy of his country because politically he does not exist. Those who *do* make a difference are the people of the cities, especially the primate cities, and, above all, the small group which rules.

To suppose that the masses in the cities will feel grateful towards us because we have improved the peasant's lot or saved him from starvation is probably unrealistic. It is hardly less so, perhaps, to suppose that the ruling groups will be moved to gratitude or respect

28

by our generosity.[35] They will assume that our actions are really selfishly motivated, and that our claims to the contrary are hypocrisy. Although they are largely Western educated, these elites do not entirely share our moral standards. In some places, the very idea of public-spiritedness is incomprehensible; actions we think noble appear as merely foolish.[36] Where nationalism is strong and ruling groups value increases in material welfare mainly for what they contribute to the prestige of the new nation, our concern for the material welfare of the individual, far from inspiring respect, may increase the ardent nationalists' contempt for us.

These considerations suggest that if aid is to have political effect it must work upon the educated class. Undertakings which stir national pride or afford direct material benefits to that class are likely to succeed best. Building an ostentatious capital city or supporting schools, theatres, and supermarkets in primate cities may do more to create politically significant sentiment in favor of the United States than much more costly projects to prevent mass starvation in the hinterland. The charge so often made, that our aid does not reach the people who need it most, is beside the point if our object is to exercise influence through gratitude and respect. For example, an observer complains that our aid program in Guatemala has been politically shortsighted *because* it has dealt with basic problems:

> The decisions as to the kinds of technical assistance to be given stemmed from a laudable but politically short-sighted philosophy that only long range and "basic" problems should be tackled— hence the great emphasis on primary education, agricultural exten-

---

[35] Among some Buddhist sects, I am told by Professor Merle Fainsod, the one who receives a gift, not the one who gives it, confers the favor.

[36] John P. Gillin, an anthropologist, says of Latin America: ". . . the notion of the 'more fortunate' elements of society actually getting down to a man-to-man basis with the 'more unfortunate' in order to help them is virtually unknown." In Lyman Bryson (ed.), *Social Change in Latin America Today* (New York: 1960), p. 36. In the Middle East, the ruling elites have not been tempted by our example to share their fabulous wealth with underlying populations. See also E. C. Banfield, *op. cit.*

29

sion, and public health. . . . Under these programs, little or no attention was paid to whether or not the segments of the population at which these efforts were aimed were politically influential.[37] But even if gratitude and respect do follow from our aid, public opinion may not favor any change of government policy towards us. One may be grateful for a gift without ceasing to dislike the policies of the giver. As Morgenthau has written:

> . . . if the recipient continues to disapprove of the political philosophy, system, and objectives of the giver, despite the aid he has received, the political effects of the aid are lost. The same is true if he remains unconvinced that the aid received is but a natural, if not inevitable, manifestation of the political philosophy, system, and objectives of the giver. Economic and technical aid remains politically ineffectual as long as the recipient says either: "Aid is good, but the politics of the giver are bad"; or: "Aid is good, but the politics of the giver—good, bad, or indifferent—have nothing to do with it."[38]

Even at its most effective, "impact" aid is not likely to change matters fundamentally. To make countries that are already friendly somewhat more so will avail us little. To bring friendly countries into a condition of "total dependency" (assuming this to be desirable) would require vast amounts of aid. To change basically the policy of uncommitted countries by this means is probably out of the question. There is a danger, too, as President Kennedy pointed out to Congress, that "if we encourage recipient countries to dramatize a series of short-term crises as a basis for our aid . . . we will dissipate our funds, our good will and our leadership."[39]

---

[37] Richard N. Adams, in *Social Change in Latin America Today* (ed. Lyman Bryson), *op. cit.,* p. 235.

[38] *Politics Among Nations,* 3d ed. (New York: 1960), p. 535. Berliner remarks that it is by no means clear that the Soviets will manage to translate good will into political advantage. India and Yugoslavia, two of the largest recipients of Soviet aid, have not been deterred from criticizing the Soviet Union., *op. cit.,* p. 180.

[39] The text of President Kennedy's message appears in the *New York Times,* March 23, 1961, p. 14. Cf. also the conclusions of Berliner with regard to Soviet aid, *op. cit.,* p. 183.

30

There is also some danger that we will create bad will by our efforts to create good will. The obligation to be grateful is often accompanied by resentment. The people of the underdeveloped countries are moved by strong feelings of both inferiority and superiority, and it would not be surprising if receiving substantial amounts of aid made many of them dislike us thoroughly.[40]

The Alternative to Aid

It is often asserted that if we do not give them aid the underdeveloped countries will eventually fall under the control of the Soviet Union and be used by it to bring about our destruction. If this is indeed the alternative, obviously we must give aid no matter how small the chances of its succeeding.

There is reason to think that this is not a realistic view of the alternative, however. For one thing, assistance for non-military purposes (the only kind of aid under discussion here) is not our sole means of preventing countries from falling under Soviet domination. Except as aid is the practical equivalent of military assistance (the recipient using it, as India does, to release for military expenditure funds that would otherwise have to be used for non-military expenditure), it is not decisive in keeping a country out of the hands of the Soviets. What *is* decisive is military assistance or the threat of it.

However, even if we gave neither aid nor military assistance, it is not likely that all of the underdeveloped countries would fall completely under Soviet control. Nationalism would be a barrier to Communist imperialism, as it has been to Western, and even if all of the countries in question did become in some sense Communist, the Kremlin probably could not impose a tight discipline

---

[40] In Mexico and Brazil, and perhaps in much smaller measure in other Latin American countries, according to Lyman Bryson, "The resentment of the debtor and the dependent have been replaced by the more vigorous and self-respecting hostility of the rival." *Social Change in Latin America Today, op. cit.,* p. 9. The extensive aid given by American Jews to Israel is said to have engendered much ill will toward the givers.

31

upon all of them in all things. Tensions like those that now exist between the Russians and the Chinese and between both the Russians and the Chinese and the Yugoslavs would certainly arise. But even if they did not—even if all of the underdeveloped countries entered fully into a monolithic bloc hostile to the United States—we would not necessarily be cut off and isolated. The monolith would find trade with us to its advantage; the present restrictions on East-West trade, it is worth noting, are mostly of our making.

Let us assume the worst, however: viz., that all of the underdeveloped countries fall completely under the control of the Soviet Union and that it uses its control to try to isolate and destroy us. Even in this event, we could probably survive and we might even prosper.

The economic consequences of such isolation would be endurable. Trade with the underdeveloped countries is relatively unimportant to us. They are comparatively cheap sources of certain raw materials, but at some additional cost we could either produce these raw materials ourselves or find substitutes for them from within our borders. The cost might be no greater than that of extending aid at the levels that would be necessary in order to achieve much by it (say $6 billion a year). If one takes into account the higher prices that we may have to pay for raw materials as the underdeveloped countries develop, it is doubtful whether "aid and trade" is a better prospect for the United States from a purely business standpoint than "no aid and no trade."[41]

Economists say that, undesirable although it would be, autarchy is a possibility for the United States. If all trade beyond our borders were to be permanently stopped, our gross national product would not necessarily be greatly reduced. We would have to get along

---

[41] Aid is sometimes justified partly on the ground that it promotes our foreign trade. Wolf, *op. cit.,* p. 281, concludes that anticipated gains from trade and increases in strategic materials supplies "should not be aid objectives because, in effect, they *can't* be." According to E. S. Mason, *op. cit.,* p. 16, "There is a little merit in this case but so little that it does not, in my opinion, justify a substantial program of foreign aid and technical assistance on these grounds alone."

without acceptable substitutes for a few things like tea, coffee, and bananas, but everything else required to sustain our economy at its present level for an indefinite time could be found within our borders. Our gross national product might even increase gradually, although not, of course, nearly as fast as it would if there were international trade.[42]

Unless the technology of war changes fundamentally, the United States and Western Europe could probably survive militarily if all of the underdeveloped countries were in Communist hands. Until we possessed a supply of atomic bombs, bases around the world were essential to our defense. They are still enormously valuable, but they are not essential.[43] We do not have them in most of the under-

---

[42] These statements are based on conversations with W. W. Leontief of Harvard. He believes that a quick transition to autarchy would create economic disruptions comparable in severity to a minor depression. For reasons given, it seems likely that the transition could occur rather slowly. See W. W. Leontief, "Les Tendences futures éventuelles des relations économiques internationales des Etats-Unis," *Revue Economique,* Paris, May 1951.

Raymond Vernon, however, sees defense advantages in husbanding scarce raw materials and, possibly, in securing a desirable dispersal pattern. "Foreign Trade and National Defense," *Foreign Affairs,* Vol. 34:1, 1955, pp. 77-88. In conversation, he has emphasized the advantage to us of the stimulation of competition from abroad, e.g., the effect on the American automobile industry of compact cars. But this, of course, arises mainly from trade with *developed* countries.

T. C. Schelling has pointed out to the writer that even if we maintained a high national income we might still lack certain materials essential to the maintenance of a competitive military position.

[43] Except for certain protected underground sites for winged Mace missiles in West Germany and in Okinawa, according to Hanson W. Baldwin, "the rest of our land-based overseas missile sites could gradually be eliminated, if the countries concerned agreed, without significant impairment of our nuclear deterrent capability." Other functions of our overseas bases and positions—protection of sea-air lines of communication, outpost and warning systems, backup points for support of limited war operations, political and psychological—are, he adds, still of high importance. *New York Times,* November 7, 1962.

developed countries (we have none in Africa south of the Sahara, in Latin America, and in India, for example), but those that we do have enable us to place our missiles close to the Soviet Union and to maintain warning and tracking stations, observation posts, and space exploration facilities where we need them. Even where we have no bases we secure a military advantage by preventing the Soviet Union from placing its bases close to us. These advantages are very substantial indeed, but we could get along without them. If we had no bases close to the Soviet Union, we could achieve the same deterrent effect, although at a greater cost, by having more missiles within our borders and on our submarines. Similarly, if the Soviets could place their missiles close to us, they would be relieved of some expense (since they would need fewer and smaller missiles) but their deterrent power would not be increased. So long as our enemies cannot prevent us from exploding a large number of nuclear weapons on their territory, we shall be safe from any attack that might threaten our national existence—as safe, that is, as anything we could do would make us—and if we maintain large conventional forces in Western Europe we can probably prevent an attack there too.[44]

Conceivably we might survive economically and militarily and yet succumb ideologically. "If the trend of the world were toward totalitarianism," a Senate subcommittee concluded after a study of aid, "then it would be only a matter of time until the free way of life in the United States would be critically threatened."[45]

Closely examined, this assertion is not as plausible as it at first appears. There is, of course, no empirical evidence to support it, and the common sense arguments against it are at least as strong as those in favor of it. Certainly the contagiousness of an idea depends to a large extent upon the susceptibility of those who are exposed to it: if, for example, cow worship were to spread around the world from India, we would be in little danger of becoming cow worship-

---

[44] The writer has benefited from discussions of these matters with Morton H. Halperin of the Center for International Affairs, Harvard University.

[45] U. S. Congress, Senate, Special Committee to Study the Foreign Aid Program, 85th Congress, 1st Session, Report No. 300, p. 8.

pers. Ideas do not infect those who find them preposterous or unintelligible. The ideologies that make sense to people suddenly emerging from pre-industrial cultures are not likely to make sense to Americans.

Confrontation by nazism and facism, far from subverting us, made us more than ever aware of our own values and more than ever determined to realize them. Such progress as we have made in recent years towards racial justice is in some measure a response to these ideological challenges. To be sure, our response might have been very different, especially in the long run, if the Nazis and Fascists had won all of Europe. But this cannot be taken for granted.

Isolationism has in recent years been the doctrine of anti-democratic and paranoid elements in our national life (although not all isolationists have been anti-democratic or paranoid), and these would no doubt be nourished by our withdrawal from the underdeveloped areas. But it is not likely that American political life would be fundamentally affected by this. If reasonable and decent people were to conclude that withdrawal was prudent, the meaning of isolationism to many people would thereby be changed, and those who were fundamentally at odds with what is reasonable and decent would have to get on the other side of the issue at once.

Withdrawal from the underdeveloped areas—i.e., liquidation of our military bases and cessation of trade—would have less effect on American cultural and intellectual life than may be supposed. The cultural and intellectual stimulation that we get from these areas is small and it does not reach us through military and trade contacts. Military and economic withdrawal, moreover, would not necessarily reduce other contacts. On the contrary, it would probably make cultural and intellectual exchange freer and easier.

That we could probably survive if all of the underdeveloped countries fell to the Communists is not, of course, a reason for letting them fall to them if we can help it—no more than that one can survive with a broken leg is a reason for letting one's leg be broken. The dangers and disadvantages of such a thing to us, even though not likely to be fatal, obviously justify very strenuous efforts—more strenuous, perhaps, than we are now making—to prevent it from happening. Even if aid is only moderately effective in keeping the underdeveloped countries out of the hands of the Communists, it is a small price to pay for a large benefit.

This, however, is very different from saying that our very existence as a nation depends upon our giving aid. Possibly we should rely entirely upon military assistance, rather than upon aid, to check Soviet imperialism. In any case, we should realize that since our survival does not depend upon the underdeveloped countries, there is some upper limit—although perhaps one so high as to be of no practical importance—to the value that contact with them has for us.

DOCTRINES JUSTIFYING AID ON OTHER THAN SECURITY GROUNDS

THOSE WHO FAVOR AID on grounds of national security usually favor it on other grounds as well. For some people, however, these other grounds are the principal, or even the sole, justification of it.

Altruism as a Basis for Aid

There are those who believe that a humanitarian desire to improve the welfare of the people of the underdeveloped areas amply justifies extensive aid and would justify it even if no security advantages could be expected from it—even if, indeed, there were some loss of security to be expected from it.[1]

The idea that a nation should promote the welfare of other nations is new in the history of political thought and of international

---

[1] The extent to which our aid is in fact altruistically motivated is not in question here, but it is worth noting that authorities disagree. According to Galbraith, "One of the things now reasonably well established in international relations is the obligation of the richer countries to help the less fortunate lands." *The Liberal Hour, op. cit.,* p. 22. But according to Mason, ". . . undertaking good works abroad without regard to national benefit is not, and never has been an objective of public policy. The morality of governments does not stretch this far." *Op. cit.,* p. 14. Viner says that although our aid has been "in some degree of a genuinely humanitarian character," (p. 178) "there is no historical experience which supports the view that national benevolence on a global scale, without expectation or prospect of a counterflow of readily visible and material benefit, is a sturdy plant which can thrive for a protracted period of time." In Hoselitz, ed., *The Progress of Under-developed Areas* (Chicago: 1952), p. 196. Wolf, *op. cit.,* p. 282, says that an effective test of a particular objective's influence is whether a different decision would be made in its absence and that by this test the humanitarian objective is in a "confirmatory and hence superfluous role." But he could have applied this criterion so as to get a different result. If there were in the world no tensions that might conceivably lead to war, would aid be entirely eliminated? The amount that would be extended under such circumstances is the measure of our purely humanitarian objective.

37

relations.[2] Statesmen have usually assumed that the object of policy is to increase the relative power of one's own nation—something that may be done by decreasing the power of others—and accordingly they have thought themselves virtuous when they have merely refrained from inflicting injuries.

As applied to aid, the doctrine of altruism presents two especially grave difficulties. One is that "doing good" may be impossible either because we do not know what is "good" or because, if we do know, we cannot bring it about and may, despite our best intentions, bring about "bad" instead. The other is that it may not be a proper function for our government to do good for people who are not its citizens.

1. It is hard to say what constitutes welfare, especially the welfare of people whose culture is radically different from our own. Our common humanity offers some guidance: food obviously serves the welfare of the starving. But even the matter of food is not so simple. By preventing starvation, we may, if we cannot at the same time reduce the rate of population growth, lower the average income and perhaps prevent the occurrence of those fundamental changes that would lead to sustained economic growth. As Viner says:

> The humanitarian approach [meaning the relief of current misery at the expense of gains that would come from increasing long-run productive capacity] in the absence of Communist ruthlessness and discipline, may lead to a race between technological progress and population growth, which is liable to be won by the latter and to culminate in universal misery, the recurrent threat of famine, and cultural and moral stagnation or even deterioration.[8]

---

[2] In *A Vindication of Natural Society*, Edmund Burke remarks that the good offices done by one nation to its neighbor would afford a very pleasing subject for history. "But, alas," he continues, "all the history of all times, concerning all nations, does not afford matter enough to fill ten pages though it should be spun out by the wire-drawing amplification of a Guicciardini himself."

[8] Hoselitz, *op. cit.*, p. 191.

We do not have to analyze the matter very far to see that "welfare" cannot be defined in purely physical terms, i.e., as amounts of food, clothing, and shelter. The untouchables of India might be "better off" if resources were used to improve their social status rather than their income. Moreover, we cannot properly compare the income of one culture with that of another or, consequently, that of a society before "modernization" with that of the same society afterward.[4] "Doing good" cannot, then, be equated with raising incomes, or with bringing about self-sustaining economic growth. The choices that we have to make when we extend aid must in the last analysis express a conception of the good life and of the good society. But if we are liberals, we believe we have no way of deciding for another culture what its ends of life should be. Does altruism demand—or even allow—that we use aid to promote freedom and democracy? Does it demand—or even allow—that we discourage the violent nationalistic attachments which stir so many people so deeply and for which they are willing to forego material improvement and even life itself?

But even if we knew in all cases what "doing good" consists of, we might not be able to do it. Despite our best efforts economic development may not occur, or, if it does occur, it may not yield the social, political, and moral benefits that are anticipated. Some countries, after suffering the agonies of change, may arrive at a condition on the whole worse than the one they left. Aid can be justified on humanitarian grounds only as it actually makes people better off; if it makes them worse off, the good intentions that motivated it are beside the point.

2. Doing good for those who are not its citizens may not be a proper function of our government. Foreign aid, like most government activities, involves taking property from some by threat of force in order to give it to others. From the 17th century, Western

---

[4] See S. Herbert Frankel, *The Economic Impact on Under-Developed Societies* (Oxford: 1953), Ch. III.

political thought has maintained that this can be justified only as it serves the common good.[5]

For example, the constitution of Massachusetts which, like the American Constitution, reflects the philosophy of Locke, declares:

> Government is instituted for the common good; for the protection, safety, prosperity, and happiness of the people; and not for the profit, honor, or private interest of any one man, family, or class of men.

According to this theory and to the constitutions which reflect it, neither state nor federal governments may take any action *all* the benefits of which are intended to accrue to foreigners (i.e., which is entirely altruistic). If governmental action to relieve starvation or to establish democracy abroad cannot be justified in terms of the welfare *of our own people,* they cannot be justified at all.

When our Government takes money from a taxpayer in New York and gives it to someone in Mississippi it does so on the ground that the nation is thereby benefited. The action is not altruistic. It is done not for the sake of the recipient but of the nation, which would suffer some loss if it were not done. In the language of economics, the transfer of income is made to prevent the occurrence of external effects which the members of the society want to avoid.

---

[5] In his *Second Treatise on Civil Government* (paragraph 131), Locke explains that since men enter into society only in order to preserve their liberty and property, the powers of civil government may rightfully "be directed to no other end but the peace, safety, and public good of the people."

Similarly, Rousseau, who carried the idea of popular rule much further, says *(The Social Contract, Book IV)* that the sovereign "cannot lay upon its subjects any burden not necessitated by the well-being of the community."

The Founding Fathers were under the influence of Locke. In *The Federalist, No. 51,* Madison justified the federal system on the grounds that it is a means of preventing government from going beyond its proper sphere, viz., "justice and the general good." Washington paraphrased Locke in his letter transmitting the draft constitution to Congress: "individuals entering into society, must give up a share of liberty *to preserve the rest.*" (Italics added.)

A gift that is genuinely altruistic, i.e., which is given not to prevent such effects but simply to make the recipient happier or better off, cannot be justified under the theory.

That it would be unconstitutional for the Federal Government to give aid if no American defense, trade, or other interests would thereby be served goes without saying. The Federal Government can exercise only the powers expressly and impliedly given to it, and doing good abroad is not one of them. But even the states, which we are in the habit of thinking can do anything not given to the Federal Government, cannot constitutionally give aid except to promote the welfare of *their own* people.[6]

It may be thought that if a large number of Americans—say a majority—want very much to have aid given through the instrumentality of the Government, the giving of it will *ipso facto* serve the common good: the common good, that is, may be defined as "whatever will serve the convenience of a large bloc of voters." But this is not consistent with the philosophy on which our Government was founded. According to this philosophy, government is justified in coercing some of its citizens (e.g., by taxing them to support aid) not in order to serve the convenience of others (even though these others may be an overwhelming majority), but only to maintain the society and to make it a good society.[7]

---

[6] This is not to say that such a measure would be found unconstitutional by the courts. As a practical matter, no one could get standing in a court to challenge such an act and in any case the decision might be in a broad sense (and perhaps a narrow one as well) political. What is meant here is that no reasonable person who takes account only of the language of the Constitution could find justification there for a measure which is not intended to serve any American interest. The writer has benefited from discussions of these matters with Professor Robert G. McCloskey of Harvard.

[7] Maintaining the society and making it a good one may perhaps require indulging the taste of some sector of the society for something (e.g., aid on purely humanitarian grounds) that does not contribute to the common good. This would be the case, for example, if not indulging the sector would alienate it from the society and thus endanger the maintenance of the society.

These considerations may appear academic in the worst sense of the word. As a practical matter, the state and federal constitutions will doubtless be got around or, if necessary, changed. Locke's philosophy, which most Americans have never heard of and many others do not accept, may be judged obsolete. Those who judge it so should be prepared, however, to offer other principles that will tell us when and how far the state may justly coerce the individual. No one believes that it may strip him of his property or his life in order to serve any and every "special interest"—not even any and every *large* one. Where, then, is the line to be drawn?

World Community as a Basis of Aid

Although academic political theorists do not seem to be much concerned about these questions, a kind of common law political theory appears to be coming into existence with regard to them. This maintains, as does the traditional theory, that government should restrict itself to serving the common good, but it defines the common good in terms that transcend the nation. A government, people seem to think, should serve the common good *of the world as a whole.*

Those who take this view think that the ultimate purpose of aid ought to be the promotion of a world community. They identify the "enlightened self-interest" of the United States with this, and are ready to sacrifice "narrow," or purely American, interests for the greater welfare of mankind. They believe that the nation state is obsolete, that we are in fact citizens of a world community, that pending the creation of a world government it is incumbent upon existing governments to act to some extent as if they were world governments (i.e., to seek to serve actively the welfare of people not their citizens), and that the United States Government, since it

---

It would be the case also if a good society were considered to be one in which sector A tolerates a government program much desired by sector B but not contributing to the common good on the understanding that at some later time sector B will tolerate one much desired by sector A but not contributing to the common good.

is the most powerful democracy, has a special obligation to lead the way.[8]

Attractive as it may be, this position is full of difficulties. World community, even if desirable, may not be a possibility. It is obvious that the world is very far from agreeing as to what constitutes its common good, and that it is entirely unwilling to let the United States decide for it. It is clear, also, that the goal of achieving world community is not perfectly compatible with that of preserving liberal democracy in the West. How much of the latter ought we to sacrifice in order to achieve something of the former? This question must also be asked with regard to other values. How far should the United States go in sacrificing its own welfare to increase that of the world as a whole? Should we, perhaps, permit immigration from the underdeveloped countries on a massive scale since that would contribute, more than anything else probably, to world welfare and world community?

Those who think that America has a responsibility to raise the level of living of mankind ought, if they are to be consistent, to think that it also has a responsibility to save the world from Communist tyranny, for that is an even worse thing. But the responsibility, if it exists, cannot stop there. Communist tyranny is not the only kind of tyranny and may not be the worst; our responsibility must therefore extend to preventing, or eradicating, all tyranny, including, of course, that which results from a people's own folly or immorality. And even here there is no reason to suppose that our responsibility ends. If we have a responsibility to prevent the people of the world from acts of political folly and immorality, do we not

---

[8] Millikan and Rostow say, p. 150, that "From the revolutionary beginnings of our history the United States has, on balance, acted in loyalty to the conception that its society has a meaning and a purpose which transcend the nation." See the proposals by Adlai Stevenson for vast international humanitarian undertakings and his question, "How can we be content in such an age to keep our political thinking within the narrow bonds of class or race or nation?" In Harlan Cleveland, ed., *The Promise of World Tensions* (New York: 1961), pp. 135-36. President Kennedy justified a proposal to use $10,000,000 to preserve Nubian temples on the upper Nile on

43

also have one to prevent them from *all* acts of folly and immorality?[9]

Those who expound the doctrine of our world responsibility ought to be prepared to acknowledge that to whatever extent we have a responsibility we must also have a right to exercise authority. The claim that one has responsibility for another implies the inequality of the two and, consequently, the right of the superior to give, and the duty of the inferior to accept, tutelage. The doctrine of American responsibility is therefore really an incomplete and confused version of the now unfashionable notion of the "white man's burden." The difference between the two doctrines—a very important one—is that whereas the old one frankly recognized the necessity of joining authority to responsibility the new one passes over the subject of authority in embarrassed silence.

The claim that we have a special responsibility for the welfare of mankind is sometimes made to rest upon our unique commitment to the principle of democracy; democracy, it is said, implies world

---

the grounds that our government has some responsibility for maintaining the civilization in which we share. "By thus contributing to the preservation of past civilizations," he said, "we will strengthen and enrich our own." See Arthur S. Miller, "Toward a Concept of National Responsibility," *The Yale Review*, LI:2 (December 1961), pp. 195-96.

[9] This sort of argument can also be used to the discomfiture of those who think that the action of a nation should always be absolutely self-interested. Since any increase in the power of any nation represents some threat (however small, remote, and contingent) to our national interest, a perfectly self-interested policy would require that we not only withhold aid but seek actively to *retard* the development of all countries, except as we anticipate some offsetting (net) advantage to us from their development. Commonsense and humanity rebel against this conclusion, of course. Even Alexander Hamilton, who was much opposed to national altruism, did not recommend a policy of absolute selfishness; policy, he said, should be regulated by national interest *as far as justice and good faith permit*. Richard B. Morris, ed., *Alexander Hamilton and the Founding of the Nation* (New York: 1958), p. 411.

If it is hard to know where to draw the line against national interest, it is no less hard to know where to draw it against national altruism and world community.

44

community, and commitment to it imposes upon us a duty to bring it about. This view has been searchingly criticized by Joseph Cropsey.[10] Democracy, he maintains, is predicated upon the belief that the enjoyment of natural rights depends absolutely on the division of mankind into nations; therefore it is not a basis for the amalgamation of the human kind into one mass, and it neither depends upon nor leads up to a fundamental moral duty. We should give aid as "a sign of grandeur," he says, not because the principle of democracy imposes any obligation to do so upon us.

Aid "Because It Is Right"

Still others maintain that the United States should give aid because the moral law requires it. According to this doctrine, the moral law places upon the rich the duty of sacrificing to help the poor. By performing this duty, the rich grow in moral worth, and they sin if they do not perform it. However, moral self improvement is not, according to the doctrine, the motive of truly charitable action. Good actions arise out of a good will, not from a calculus of spiritual gains and losses, and therefore a rich nation should help poor ones not in order to improve the quality of its own national life but simply (as President Kennedy said in his inaugural address) "because it is right."

This doctrine assumes what many Americans do not believe: that ethical imperatives get their force from nature or God's will and not from mere convention. But the doctrine also is open to grave objection by those who *do* believe in natural law. For the obligation to act morally is placed upon *persons,* not upon entities like governments or corporations—entities which, as someone said, have neither souls to be saved nor backsides to be kicked.

Aid given by a government is morally significant only insofar as it expresses the intention of "persons" as distinguished from "roles." Conceivably the rulers of a nation, acting not as "persons" (i.e., out of their own good wills) but as "officials" (i.e., as role incumbents

---

[10] Cropsey's paper is to appear in a volume edited by Robert A. Goldwin, *op. cit.*

serving the state), might give extensive aid without their citizens knowing or caring what was being done in their names, or perhaps even over the lively opposition of most of the citizens. If people are coerced into "giving" or if their money is given without their knowledge, the gift is morally meaningless. One who taxes Peter to give to Paul cannot gain moral credit either for himself or for Peter. Insofar as aid is to be justified by the obligation to be charitable, it must be voluntary. To some extent it is voluntary even when provided by legislative appropriation: some taxpayers want to act charitably through the instrumentality of the government. Others, however, do not. To the extent that a government appropriation takes more from some (and less from others) than they would freely choose to give, it does not apply the principle of charity.

It is pertinent to observe that design of an aid program that will effectively attain the objective of charity is a relatively simple matter. It is easier to intend good than actually to do it. From the moral standpoint (and, incidentally, from that of national self improvement also), it makes no difference if the actual effect of aid is to make the recipients worse off. Even if our greatest efforts achieved nothing or actually made matters worse, our good will would, as Kant said, "like a jewel, still shine by its own light." Had the Wayfarer died from being moved, the Samaritan would have been no less good, provided, of course, that he was sufficiently ignorant of the probable consequences of his action. According to St. Thomas, *Eventus sequens non facit actum malum qui erat bonus, nec bonum qui erat malus.*

Aid for National Self-Improvement

It is sometimes argued that we ought to do good to others for the sake of improving ourselves. For example, Millikan and Rostow say that, after national security, the justification for aid is that "American society is at its best when wrestling with the positive problems of building a better world." We need, they say, "the challenge of world development to keep us from the stagnation of smug prosperity."[11]

---

[11] *Op. cit.,* pp. 7 and 8.

46

To the extent that our motive is of this kind, the philosophical problems just discussed do not arise. This is *seeming* altruism, not the real thing, because here the reason for giving is to secure advantages to the giver.

The anticipated improvements in the quality of our national life are of two main kinds. An extensive aid program, some think, would activate and strengthen the bonds attaching the individual to the collectivity. By being drawn into a great national effort the individual would be made more aware of the values that are central to the life of the society and would be distracted somewhat from the frivolous and demoralizing influences that the private sector of the economy—especially the mass media—ceaselessly plays upon him. Foreign aid, like public expenditures in general, would thus be a moral equivalent of war: it would moralize and socialize the individual by asserting social values over private whims and tastes. This doctrine implies an aid program of a kind that would give Americans a strong sense of involvement in collective action.[12]

Some will say that the Government has no right to manipulate the national mood or to remake the national culture; that in a democracy government ought to be the product of public opinion, not the creator of it. There is much to be said for this view, and yet it seems clear the Government must concern itself with national mood to the extent that "leadership" requires; moreover, if the purpose of the state is to promote the common good—i.e., to create conditions leading to the formation of a good society—then it must also in certain circumstances concern itself with the quality of the culture. The real questions, therefore, seem to be two: whether there is in fact the cause for concern about the state of the national mind that the critics of mass culture and of private enterprise assert, and whether, if there is, an aid program is a suitable means of securing

---

[12] The Peace Corps, Richard Rovere reports from Washington, "is at least as much an effort to dissolve apathy and boredom in this country as it is a scheme for improving the conditions of life in the underdeveloped nations. It is an attempt to revive and find a fitting use for American idealism." *The New Yorker*, March 25, 1961, p. 131.

47

the closer attachment to collective values that is necessary. Both of these questions are, of course, open to much dispute.

The other main way in which, according to some, an extensive aid program would improve the quality of our national life is by stimulating and inspiring the elites within our society. Aid, it is said, would release energies among us just as it would release them in the underdeveloped countries. According to Myrdal:

> Not merely to save the world, but primarily to save our own souls, there should again be dreamers, planners, and fighters, in the midst of our nations, who would take upon themselves the important social function in democracy of raising our sights—so far ahead that their proponents again form a definite minority in their nations and avoid the unbearable discomfort for reformers of a climate of substantial agreement. This is only possible if they enlarge the scope of their interests to encompass the world scene. They must again become internationalists, as they were when the reform movements started in the wake of the Enlightenment and the French revolution.[13]

As this suggests, giving reformers vast resources to work with would tend to increase both their influence and that of the very idea of reform; the effect of extensive aid on reformers and on reform might be something like that of the development of nuclear power on scientists and on science. Looking at the matter from a slightly different perspective, aid may also be valued as one of the activities which will serve to occupy the growing leisure of an affluent middle class in a society having a strong bent towards "service" and organizational behavior.

---

[13] Gunnar Myrdal, *An International Economy* (New York: 1956), p. 322.

AID DOCTRINE AND DEMOCRACY

AFTER CONSIDERING ALL of the arguments that have been brought forward, a reasonable man might still conclude that we ought to give extensive aid to certain countries—much more of it, perhaps, than we are now giving. Any decision must turn on probability judgments and value judgments that are highly subjective. That a given country will or will not develop economically, that its development will or will not lead to peace and democracy, that its government or public opinion can or cannot be influenced to our advantage—these are all questions about which we may form judgments more or less intelligently, but they are not ones about which we can get reliable answers. And even if we knew the probabilities exactly, we might still differ profoundly about the amount of risk that the United States should accept.

That many people favor giving extensive aid does not, then, require explanation. But that almost no "serious" writers oppose giving it or even have serious doubts about it; that after more than ten years the theory of aid has not been worked out and the arguments for it have not been subjected to hard scrutiny, and that (to the extent such a test is possible) the factual premises of aid doctrines have not been tested—all this *does* require explanation.

The Character of the Discussion

The American theory and practice of foreign aid, as Hans J. Morgenthau has said, "has derived by and large from certain unexamined assumptions that are part of the American folklore of politics."[1] The most influential writings are hardly more than collections of clichés strung together with rhetorical flourishes. They are full of sweeping statements that turn out on examination to be either meaningless or without any supporting evidence. Nevertheless, their tone is always

---

[1] *The New Atlantic Community.* Text of the Introductory Report to the Fifth Congress of *"Il Mulino"* on the Foreign Policy of the United States and the Responsibilities of Europe, Societá Editrice Il Mulino, Bologna, 1961, p. 16.

confident and often hortatory or polemical. The authors do not acknowledge that they have nothing but common sense to go on, if indeed they have that, or that reasonable men may hold opinions very different from theirs. Instead of laboring to make complex what appears to be simple, a task scholars should find congenial, writers on aid, including some of the "serious" ones, try to make matters seem simpler than they are.[2]

Most of the "serious" writing does not clarify the ends of policy. We may be told that the end is to promote freedom and democracy, but the concrete meaning of these ends and the relation between them and others like "national interest" or "national survival" (whatever these may mean) is left unexplained. Economists often ignore the political objectives of aid and treat economic improvement as if it were always the only value to be considered.[3] It is especially

---

[2] It is "serious" *public* discussion that is here being criticized. Discussions within officialdom have apparently been immensely more sophisticated. One which has appeared in print is 86th Congress, 1st Session, House Doc. No. 215, Part 2, "Conclusions Concerning the Mutual Security Program" (1959). This consists of papers written for the Draper Committee. See especially those by Paul H. Nitze and John H. Ohly.

[3] For example, Benjamin Higgins in a well-known textbook: "What is important, however, is that neither private investment nor foreign aid be used—or even appear to be used—for any purpose other than raising total output in the country where the investment is made." *Economic Development* (New York: 1959), p. 628.

Hollis B. Chenery, an economist who is a high official of the aid agency, concedes that the threat of a Communist take-over may necessitate giving aid for purposes that contribute very little to long-term development. But for him the justification of this politically motivated, short-run aid is not some immediate advantage of the United States but rather the success of the long-term development program: "It cannot be said that such a use is never as desirable as aid that produces long-term development, *because, if the political diagnosis is correct, the country's development would be set back for a number of years if the aid were not given."* Italics added.

Chenery defines the long-term objective of aid as the production of self-sustaining economic and political evolution. A careful reading of his paper suggests, however, that for him, as for Millikan and Rostow, "economic

50

hard, apparently, for writers on aid to believe that technological improvements may on balance be undesirable.[4] Writers on aid rarely give any consideration to alternative ways of achieving their ends (e.g., "one way free trade" is not considered by those who favor loans and grants). Sometimes they have no means to suggest for attaining ends that they say are crucial (e.g., Millikan and Rostow do not tell how to bring about the social, political, and psychological changes they say are indispensable). They seldom recognize that the ends appropriate in one country or culture may not be in another, and that, even in those instances where the same ends are appropriate in different countries, the means required to achieve them may be entirely different. Nor do they usually acknowledge that in choosing one set of ends and means we forego the possibly greater advantages associated with others that are incompatible, and that therefore we should decide in such a way as to "balance our margins," i.e., secure the greatest *total* return in terms of the several values (e.g., economic development vs. "impact") among which our stock of resources is to be rationed.

The writing on aid not only lacks the systematic relating of means and ends that is the defining characteristic of rational planning, but much of it conceals the hard problems of choice behind a fog of moralizing. By "moralizing" is meant advocacy, as a basis for action, of moral principles that do not take account of elements of the situation which render them inapplicable or inappropriate. The moralizer averts his gaze from those features of the real situation that constitute the crux of the problem and then, unhampered, tells us

and political" evolution is concretely indistinguishable from "economic" evolution. His paper appears in the collection edited by Robert A. Goldwin, *op. cit.*

[4] The M.I.T. group thinks "A major breakthrough for development would be the creation and production by the millions of a cheap long-lived battery radio or television set designed to bring mass communication into villages, bypassing the prerequisites of literacy and electricity" and that "American effort can help." *The Emerging Nations, op. cit.*, p. 109. That "bypassing literacy" may make it impossible to govern the world *decently* is not considered.

how to act in a world different from the one in which we must act. For example, he warns severely against extending aid to corrupt tyrannies or reactionary ruling oligarchies. This would be good advice if the choice were really between a corrupt tyranny and an honest democracy. Alas, this is seldom the choice, and when it is, the advice is usually not needed. The real problem exists when we must choose between a corrupt tyranny and a Communist one—and here the advice of the moralizer is at best confusing and at worst wrong. He refuses, however, to acknowledge the real problem. If it is pointed out to him that supporting a corrupt tyranny may in some circumstances be necessary, he replies blandly that "the proper and the practical courses coincide."[5]

Similarly, the moralizer cannot see, or else refuses to acknowledge, the tension between the goal of world community and the goal of preserving democracy in the West, or the tension between the security interests of the United States and the development needs of the underdeveloped countries. "As long as our policies are designed to help these societies develop in directions which meet the real interests of their own people," he tells us, "our political and our moral interests coincide."[6]

Sometimes moralizing is half hidden behind an affectation of political realism. For example, Eugene R. Black, president of the World Bank, tells us that by sacrificing our present political advantage to promote long-term economic development we will serve our *real* political interests.[7] And Reinhold Niebuhr, who is known as a politi-

---

[5] J. K. Galbraith, *The Liberal Hour, op. cit.,* p. 23.

[6] Millikan and Blackmer, eds., *op. cit.,* p. 145.

[7] "The issue is this: Are the political interests of the West better served by administering economic aid in an effort to outbid the Russians for public favor in the underdeveloped world? Or are they better served by administering aid with the single-minded purpose of providing something which the underdeveloped countries require for more rapid growth? If the West is to use aid primarily to court the favor of the underdeveloped countries and to woo them away from the Communists, it should be recognized that aid can all too easily play into the Communists' hands. It can all too easily result in channeling resources into uneconomic projects and programs, thereby

cal realist, explains that the art of statecraft is to find "the point of concurrence" between the national and the international common good; apparently he is confident that there is such a point, for he goes on to say that "this policy means that we must try to persuade the nation that what is good for the alliance of the free nations is good for our own Nation *in the long run.*"[8] Such statements conjure the crucial problems of choice out of existence by making it appear that conflicts of interest only *seem* to exist—that "in the long run" there are no conflicts and "the proper and the practical courses coincide," presumably at the "point of concurrence."

This mentality, evident in most of the writing on aid, ignores the very facts that constitute the problem: that vast areas of the world show little prospect of achieving self-sustaining economic growth or of governing themselves reasonably well within the foreseeable future; that development, when it does take place, is as likely to be inspired by blood and hate as by peace and rational management; that the development of the underdeveloped countries may not on balance be in the interest of the United States or, indeed, of civilization; and that the measures most effective in relieving misery and promoting economic growth are in general least effective in serving the urgent necessities of the West. Instead of facing up to these

---

subverting the economics of the underdeveloped countries rather than strengthening them. Surely, the choice should be to contribute something that is really required for economic growth. This may mean that in the propaganda battle the West will often have to settle for letting virtue be its own reward; however, such a settlement is, I suggest, quite in keeping with the real security interests of the West." *The Diplomacy of Economic Development* (Cambridge: 1960), p. 46.

Secretary of State Dean Rusk has also taken this position. Too often in the past, he said, aid has been given to counter Communist aid or to save an economy from imminent collapse. The fostering of long-term development "must be the paramount goal in the granting of aid in the Sixties." Speech on May 3, 1961.

[8] Reinhold Niebuhr, *Our Moral and Spiritual Resources for International Cooperation,* U.S. State Department, International Organization and Conference Series IV, February 1956.

tragic facts and endeavoring to frame a course of action that is workable and represents the least among evils for us and for mankind, writers on aid generally proffer a few sententious principles of everyday morality and issue stern warnings against using aid for political purposes.[9]

When policy based upon such misconceptions fails, the moralizer knows whom to blame. Not, surely, anyone in the underdeveloped countries—not even if the obvious cause of the trouble is there. Still less those like himself upon whose naive and sentimental notions the policy was based. The fault, he says, is with the United States; it was not generous enough, or not tactful enough, or not firm

---

[9] Lucian W. Pye concludes from a brilliant comparison of American and Soviet aid doctrines that many of the defects of ours arise from its basically apolitical character: "Out of the logic of politics they [the Soviets] have been able to realize a coherence between ends and means, between goals and techniques. We, on the other hand, in denying the sovereignty of politics, find ourselves without an explicit method for dealing rigorously with the relationships between goals and techniques. We have built up our doctrines as though little attention need be given to the links between our practices and the end values we seek, or between economic aid and our other instruments of policy.

"Our difficulty seems to arise, in part, from an uneasiness about the propriety of discussing openly the relationship between our values and the available means for influencing events. We are disturbed by our traditional uncertainties about the concept of manipulation in human affairs. A further complication is our feeling that in speaking across the gap in technology between our society and the underdeveloped countries, it is improper and indelicate to discuss values and objectives. Instead, we behave as though the situation calls for innocent discussion about impersonal and technical matters.

"By putting off to the side the crucial problem of how to relate our objectives and our practices to each other, we have allowed the center of the stage to be taken over by supposedly technical economic considerations. As a consequence we have made techniques into the molders of doctrine rather than treating them as the servants of doctrine. We have built our ideology by pushing beyond the realm of its relevance the analytical reasoning of economics. In so moving from technique to doctrine we have been easily captivated by a false sense of realism." "Soviet and American Styles in Foreign Aid," *Orbis*, Vol. IV:2, 1960, pp. 171-72.

enough,[10] or it did not organize and plan effectively.[11] That the failure may have been unavoidable, the natures of givers and receivers being what they are, is a possibility that escapes him altogether. "Giving and receiving can be attended by increasing self-respect and friendship," he says categorically, and from this concludes that we should "manage to make the receiver feel he is a partner whose growing strength is important to [our] own welfare."[12]

---

[10] Some American writers on aid think this country at fault for not attaching stringent conditions to aid, as if attaching conditions were a sure way to solve the problems which necessitate the aid. For example, the Secretary of State recently (May 31, 1961) told the Senate Foreign Relations Committee that "self-help" should be an "insistent" condition of aid; Millikan and Rostow (*op. cit.*, p. 129) would apply "tough criteria of productivity" (as well as require that national development goals be democratically established!), and Galbraith (*Foreign Affairs*, April 1961) insists that recipients plan and carry out sweeping social and political reforms. These principles, which have been much emphasized in the Alliance for Progress, ignore the obvious fact that it is the inability, or unwillingness, of these countries to do these things that constitutes the very problem. If the conditions were taken seriously, the countries most in need of aid would not be able to qualify for it.

[11] Along with declarations of good intentions (declarations made, however, by the giver rather than the receivers), American writers on aid place great confidence in organizational arrangements and planning. For example, Galbraith, after finding at least four "crucial" prerequisites of development missing in most of the poor countries (see footnote 8, first section), is led not to question the possibility of a successful aid program (the voters, he says, did not intend inaction when they put the new administration into office) but instead to propose that the underdeveloped countries be required to make Positive Development Plans. "By establishing targets and agreeing upon the steps to achieve them," he says, "all the barriers to development will be brought into view." *Ibid,* p. 454. It does not occur to him, apparently, that factors more fundamental than organization may have kept the barriers from coming into view or that, even if the barriers are now brought into view, it may be impossible to eliminate them.

[12] W. Averell Harriman, "Leadership in World Affairs," *Foreign Affairs,* Vol. 32:4, 1954, p. 535.

Why Aid Doctrine Is Confused

The unsatisfactory state of the theory of aid is to be explained in part by the variety of the situations in which it has been expected to play a part.[13] When the war ended, it meant relief to the occupied countries, and its justification was obvious. When hastening the restoration of the European economy appeared desirable, the meaning of aid changed accordingly. The success of the Marshall Plan encouraged efforts to assist the underdeveloped countries, and so there was a further drastic change in the meaning of aid. Before a new rationale for it had been found—indeed, before the necessity of finding one was fully realized—the Korean War broke out and its meaning changed again, this time to "defense support." When the strategic situation was further changed by the development of long-range missiles, the rationale of aid needed to be modified accordingly. Since ideas, as well as the institutions that embody them, often long outlast the circumstances that give rise to them, it is not surprising that present day aid doctrine consists largely of left-overs and hand-me-downs.

This, however, does not entirely account for the deficiencies of aid doctrine. In particular, it does not account for its optimistic, moralizing, self-deprecating, and apolitical (even anti-political) character, or for the absence from it of rigorous criticism and dissent. To account for these deficiencies, it is necessary to look at certain features of our political system.

Most matters are decided politically by competition of interests.[14] The system gives those who have something at stake in a particular matter a great deal of incentive to exert influence. This leads them to work up the strongest possible case for their interest and to assert it vigorously; it leads them also to search for weaknesses in

---

[13] See Lorna and Felix Morley, *The Patchwork History of Foreign Aid* (Washington: American Enterprise Association, 1961).

[14] By an "interest" is meant an end which an actor seeks to attain for his own benefit rather than for the benefit of the whole society. A "principle," by contrast, is a statement about what is believed to be good for the whole society.

the arguments of their opponents and to call these to public attention. Competition of interests tends, therefore, to bring a wide range of policy alternatives into consideration and to expose each of them to searching criticism. When, by contrast, principles, as distinguished from interests, are at stake, the incentive to exercise influence is usually much less and the amount of information and criticism generated in the course of discussion is correspondingly less. When the principles are ones about which there is general agreement, the amount of information and criticism is likely to be at a minimum.[15] This has been the case in the discussion of aid. Some interests have indeed been active, but these (mainly farmers and manufacturers wanting subsidized markets) have almost all been in favor of aid and therefore have had no incentive to analyze it critically. For the most part, decisions about aid have been based on principles— principles about which there was general agreement—and not on the outcome of competition among interests. For this reason, aid has not been discussed as informatively as have those other matters— the farm problem, for example—about which a variety of powerful interests contend.

Because it concerns principles much more than interests, aid as an issue is peculiarly serviceable to the President. One of the most conspicuous features of our political system is the necessity for him to gather in one way or another enough influence to mitigate the extreme decentralization of formal authority contrived by the Founding Fathers. In former times, state and local political machines and the patronage and logrolling prerogatives of the Presidency went far toward giving him the influence he needed. These are still important, but much less so, and the amount of power the President needs to govern the country has meanwhile greatly increased. It is becoming ever more necessary, therefore, for him to enlarge his power by appealing directly to the public through press and television. Sir Henry Sumner Maine observed three-quarters of a century

---

[15] This argument is elaborated in E. C. Banfield, *Political Influence* (Glencoe: 1961), Ch. 12. See also Willmoore Kendall, "The Two Majorities," *Midwest Journal of Political Science,* Vol. IV:4, 1960, pp. 317-45.

ago that to Party and Corruption, the influences which had hitherto shown themselves capable of bringing the masses of men under civil discipline, democracy was adding a third: "generalization, the trick of rapidly framing, and confidently uttering, general propositions on political subjects."

> General formulas, which can be seen on examination to have been arrived at by attending only to particulars few, trivial, or irrelevant, are turned out in as much profusion as if they dropped from an intellectual machine; and debates in the House of Commons may be constantly read, which consisted wholly in the exchange of weak generalities and strong personalities. On a pure Democracy this class of general formulas has a prodigious effect. Crowds of men can be got to assent to general statements, clothed in striking language, but unverified and perhaps incapable of verification; and thus there is formed a sort of sham and pretence of concurrent opinion. There has been a loose acquiescence in a vague proposition, and then the People, whose voice is the voice of God, is assumed to have spoken. Useful as it is to democracies, this levity of assent is one of the most enervating of national habits of mind.[16]

As the power of our central government comes to depend more and more upon appeals from the President to the public, "generalizations" must be manufactured at an ever faster rate and on an ever larger scale. Great formulas for solving the nation's and the world's problems are now an indispensable means of generating the popular support that is required to govern the country. The Cold War is, naturally, the principal subject matter about which "generalizations" can be developed. The question of the proper role of our country in world development is another, however, and if the Cold War were to end it would be one of the few good ones left.[17]

---

[16] Sir Henry Sumner Maine, *Popular Government* (New York: 1886), pp. 107-08.

[17] "The United States is now within sight of solutions to the range of issues which have dominated its political life since 1865. Our central problem has been to reconcile the fact of industrialization with the abiding principles of democracy. The farm problem, the status of big business in a democratic society, the status and responsibilities of organized labor, the avoidance of

It is not hard to understand why generalizations about foreign aid have popular appeal. We are a nation of activists; we see the relative power of our nation declining and great masses of the world's people suffering chronic poverty while we enjoy unparalleled prosperity. Our impulse is to do something at once. Under the circumstances, about the only thing we can do is to give money. There may be little reason to hope that giving it will improve the situation, but doing so to some extent satisfies our urge for action and it also helps to relieve our feelings of guilt at being rich when others are poor. Moreover, it is cheap, since we do not give up anything really valuable—only money.

There is also at work, however, a much more fundamental and pervasive trait of our national mind. We have always believed that we are the fortunate possessors of political truth, and that other nations will, in time, have to imitate us, or be converted by us, in order to be saved. We have, as Kennneth W. Thompson has said, always abhorred force, distrusted diplomacy, and put our faith in comprehensive formulas for solving the world's problems while exhibiting a "deeply ingrained tendency to speak in large and absolute terms" and to take to all questions a good-and-bad, right-and-wrong approach.[18] Our faith that democracy can regenerate the world without coercion has led us to try one legal or institutional

---

extreme cyclical unemployment, social equity for the Negro, the provision of equal education opportunity, the equitable distribution of income—none of all these great issues is fully resolved; but a national consensus on them exists within which we are clearly moving forward as a nation. The achievement of this consensus absorbed much of the nation's creativeness and idealism over the past ninety years. If we continue to devote our attention in the same proportion to domestic issues as in the past, we run the danger of becoming a bore to ourselves and the world. We shall be quarreling over increasingly smaller margins, increasingly narrower issues. While enjoying the material fruits of a rich and complacent society, we shall become progressively isolated from the vital issues of the world." Millikan and Rostow, *op. cit.*, p. 194.

[18] Kenneth W. Thompson, *Christian Ethics and the Dilemmas of Foreign Policy* (Durham, N. C.: 1959), pp. 58-59.

gadget after another. As Thompson, describing the American view of the world after 1914, puts it:

> . . . War was widely attributed to the wickedness of governments and, more specifically, to the nefarious role of secret treaties. A philosophy of international relations was born and flourished which because of its simplicity and directness engendered widespread popular appeal—an appeal that continues to the present day. It was a philosophy which in a spirit of buoyant optimism looked to democracy and national self-determination as twin sources of international peace and order. The creation of popular regimes on the Anglo-American model throughout the world was heralded as the sure corrective to those harsh conflicts that for centuries had wracked international life. Once the numerous subject peoples had achieved political societies reflecting the popular will, their ancient rivalries with "oppressor" states and the struggles between conflicting dominions warring over territorial claims would come to an end. The unquenchable faith of contemporary Western *homo sapiens* in man's potentialities for progress spiraling ever upward found expression in assurances that a brave new world merely awaited the fulfillment of these goals.
>
> However, faith in the future has had its roots not only in democracy and national self-determination; it also resides in the confidence that novel international institutions have rendered diplomacy obsolete. Implicit here is a belief that the certainty of progress is waiting at the other end of a charter, a constitution, or a court judgment. The United Nations emerges in the minds of some of its American champions as an organization that may confidently be expected to do away with alliances, balance of power, secret diplomacy, and state rivalries.[19]

History, Thompson says, has dealt harshly with these views and our faith in them has been rudely shaken. He forgets, apparently, about foreign aid. The same old zeal to make the world safe for democracy is expressed anew in this. Aid is for the 1960's what arbitration and the World Court were for the 1920's, and what the United Nations was for the decade just passed.

---

[19] *Ibid.*, p. 79.

The Dangerous Goodness of Democracy

The reason for our inveterate devotion to these millennial ideas is to be found in the nature of our kind of democracy.[20] Ours is the only country in which the public at large participates actively in the daily conduct of government; it is the only one in which the opinions of amateurs on foreign affairs are listened to by statesmen and taken seriously by them; consequently it is the only one in which the moral standards of the general public are decisive in the making of policy.[21]

The moral standards of a people are necessarily very different from those of its statesmen. A statesman learns early that it is his duty to act according to the rules of virtue, not those of goodness.[22] Goodness pertains to persons, and is expressed in their everyday relations; it calls for (among other things) kindness, liberality, compassion, and the doing of justice. Virtue, by contrast, pertains to statesmen and is expressed in the actions by which they protect good citizens from both bad citizens and foreign enemies. Virtue has little to do with goodness, and may be entirely at odds with it in concrete cases; frequently the statesman must act unjustly or without kindness in order to protect the society—he must, in short, be virtuous but not good. As Churchill has written, "The Sermon on the

---

[20] "Democracy" means government by the people, i.e., a political order in which power is widely distributed. In some democracies, e.g., the British, the people exercise their power mainly by giving or withholding consent at infrequent intervals; in others e.g., our own, they exercise it by participating continuously and intimately in the day-to-day conduct of affairs. What is said about the dangerous goodness of "our kind of democracy" has little application to the other kind, in which the citizen is willing to leave the management of public affairs—and above all foreign affairs—to his elected rulers.

[21] Chester Bowles, justifying the "tough-minded" approach recommended by him on August 14, 1962 (see footnote 27, first section), said: "It has been pre-tested over a period of years before many audiences in most states of the Union."

[22] This discussion of goodness and virtue draws upon Leo Strauss, *Thoughts on Machiavelli* (Glencoe: 1958), pp. 264-65.

61

Mount is the last word in Christian ethics. Everyone respects the Quakers. Still, it is not on these terms that Ministers assume their responsibilities of guiding states."[23]

Nations, the orthodoxy of political realism tells us, do what their vital interests require, however immoral those things may be. This may be true of nations that are governed by statesmen free to act as their judgment dictates. It is not, however, true of those governed, as ours is, by public opinion. A nation governed by public opinion may act contrary to its fundamental moral standards when swept by passion or when self-deceived. But it does not act so from deliberation or calculation. What is more, it is strongly impelled to express in action the *positive* principles of its morality, i.e., its goodness.

American foreign policy has long been heavily tainted with goodness, and our country, consequently, has frequently acted against its own interests. Political realists, overlooking the difference between the morality of peoples and that of statesmen, have usually regarded American goodness as mere hypocrisy and have looked in the usual places for the "real" reasons of national interest that they were sure must exist.[24]

---

[23] Winston S. Churchill, *The Gathering Storm* (Boston: 1948), p. 320.

[24] Niebuhr, for example, finds that the Spanish-American War offers "some of the most striking illustrations of the hypocrisy of governments." He marvels that a man as intelligent as Walter Hines Page could speak of the war as a chance to clean out bandits, yellow fever, malaria, and hookworm and to make the country safe for life and investment and orderly self-government, and that he could write: "What we did in Cuba might thus be made the beginning of a new epoch in history, conquest for the sole benefit of the conquered." He sneers at McKinley's "hypocrisy" in claiming that it came to him while on his knees in prayer "that there was nothing left for us to do but to take them all, and to educate the Filipinos, and uplift and civilize and Christianize them, and by God's grace do the very best we could by them." *Moral Man and Immoral Society* (New York: 1960), pp. 98-102.

Perhaps there was an element of self-deception in what Page and McKinley said, but there is a world of difference morally between self-

62

The optimistic, moralizing, and apolitical nature of American aid doctrine is a characteristic expression of this goodness. Goodness inclines men to have faith in each other, or at any rate to give each other the benefit of the doubt; public opinion therefore takes a compassionate and hopeful view of the prospects for growth and development however discouraging may be the underlying realities of the situation. It is by moralizing that one appeals to goodness; the discussion of the truly hard problems of choice, viz., those in which the principles of goodness will not suffice as criteria, presupposes virtue rather than goodness. Action that is apolitical in the sense that it sees in the situation not the necessity of a struggle for power but rather the opportunity to cooperate in the realization of shared ends is consistent with goodness but not necessarily with virtue.

To know when and on what terms to subordinate goodness to virtue requires high intellectual and moral powers as well as much experience in making—and in taking responsibility for—decisions in important public matters. Few citizens can have all of these qualifications. The citizen, moreover, knows that his views will count only along with those of millions of other citizens, and so he may not trouble to go deeply enough into any public question to see its full moral complexity. Hence his confidence that the proper and the practical courses will coincide and that great affairs of states may be decided by the standards that apply in everyday life.

A public, moreover, cannot deliberately transgress the principles of its morality. Societies are held together by attachment to common values, especially ones that are held sacred. To call such values publicly into question, to consider openly the expediency of transgressing them, and then actually to do so (even though in order to realize other values) would profane and destroy the values and so

---

deception and hyprocrisy, i.e., the deception of others in order to gain one's ends. Moreover, it is not clear in what sense they were self-deceived. They seem to have had the same confident intention of doing good that the present-day advocates of aid have, and, as Niebuhr himself says (p. 102), the United States did in fact do much to improve education and sanitation in the places it conquered.

weaken the mystic bonds that hold the society together. Such a thing could happen only if the values of the society had already lost their sacredness, and if, therefore, the society was in process of disintegration. A healthy society cannot subject its ultimate moral code to detached, rational scrutiny. If its code is to be scrutinized at all, the scrutinizing must be done by an elite set apart for the purpose—one which, like a bomb decontamination squad, possesses both a specialized skill and a willingness to expose itself to risk for the sake of the society. The professional statesman belongs to this elite.[25]

Much as we may wish it, the world cannot be ruled according to the Sermon on the Mount or the principles of the Quakers, and a determined effort to rule it so may lead to disaster. The goodness and optimism inseparable from democracy represent a great peril. The peril would be somewhat less if we gave our statesmen wide discretion in foreign affairs, as the other democracies do. Our statesmen, however, are trained to goodness, and they are selected for it rather than for virtue. Our tradition and the exigencies of our political system, moreover, tend more and more to subordinate them to public opinion. Confident that its goodness is the world's best hope, American public opinion reaches out eagerly for wider power in world affairs ("accepts responsibility for world leadership" is the cant phrase), thereby engendering—the United Nations is a case in point—ever more goodness in places where virtue is required, and thereby increasing ever more the incongruity between the reality of the situation in which we must act and the moral principles upon which our action is based. It is quite possible that the American

---

[25] Saint Augustine, after remarking that a judge may torture and condemn an innocent man "not with any intention of doing harm, but because his ignorance compels him, and because human society claims him as a judge" concludes that although we may acquit the judge of malice "we must none the less condemn human life as miserable." If the judge must subordinate goodness to virtue, he ought at least to regret the necessity. "Surely it were proof of more profound considerateness and finer feeling were he to shrink from his own implication in that misery; and had he any piety about him, he would cry to God, 'From my necessities deliver Thou me.'" *The City of God,* Modern Library Edition, pp. 682-83.

people may be persuaded that the indiscriminate use of aid is folly (events may persuade them of this even though their leaders tell them the contrary). But this will not necessarily improve our foreign policy very greatly. The millenial and redemptionist character of that policy will not necessarily be changed thereby; if the American people cannot express their goodness through foreign aid they will doubtless find some other way of expressing it. To the extent that public opinion rules, our policy will reflect goodness. This is a cause for concern because goodness is, by its very nature, incapable of understanding its own inadequacy as a principle by which to govern relations among states.

SELECTED BIBLIOGRAPHY

Books and Pamphlets

Galbraith, J. K. *Economic Development in Perspective* (Cambridge: Harvard University Press, 1962).
Goldwin, Robert A. ed. "Essays on Foreign Aid Doctrines" (title as yet unannounced), (Chicago: Rand-McNally and Co.).
Liska, George. *The New Statecraft* (Chicago: University of Chicago Press, 1960).
Millikan, Max F. and Rostow, W. W. *A Proposal* (New York: Harper & Brothers, 1957).
Millikan, Max F. and Blackmer, D. L. M. eds. *The Emerging Nations* (Boston: Little, Brown and Co., 1961).
Niebuhr, Reinhold. *Our Moral and Spiritual Resources for International Cooperation.* U. S. Department of State, International Organization and Conference Series IV, February 1956.
Schelling, T. S. in the American Assembly. *International Stability and Progress,* 1957.
Wolf, Charles Jr. *Foreign Aid, Theory and Practice in Southern Asia* (Princeton: Princeton University Press, 1960).

Articles

Brzezinski, Zbigniew. "The Politics of Underdevelopment," *World Politics,* Vol. IX, No. 1, 1956.
Galbraith, J. K. "A Positive Approach to Foreign Aid," *Foreign Affairs,* Vol. 39, No. 3, 1961.
Galbraith, J. K. "Rival Economic Theories in India," *Foreign Affairs,* July 1958.
Friedman, Milton. "Foreign Economic Aid: Means and Objectives," *The Yale Review,* Summer 1958.
Harriman, W. Averell. "Leadership in World Affairs," *Foreign Affairs,* Vol. 32, No. 4, 1954.
Lilienthal, David. "Needed: A New Credo for Foreign Aid," *New York Times Magazine,* June 26, 1960.
Wright, David McCord. "Stages of Growth vs. the Growth of Freedom," *Fortune,* December 1959.

Government Documents

86th Congress, 1st Session, House Document No. 215. Part 2, "Conclusions Concerning the Mutual Security Program," 1959. See especially the papers by Paul H. Nitze and John H. Ohly.

PUBLICATIONS

STUDIES

The Rescue of the Dollar, *Wilson E. Schmidt*—1963

The Role of Gold, *Arthur Kemp*—1963

Pricing Power and "Administrative" Inflation—Concepts, Facts and Policy Implications, *Henry W. Briefs*—1962

Depreciation Reform and Capital Replacement, *William T. Hogan*—1962

The Federal Antitrust Laws, *Jerrold G. Van Cise*—1962

Consolidated Grants: A Means of Maintaining Fiscal Responsibility, *George C. S. Benson* and *Harold F. McClelland*—1961

Inflation: Its Causes and Cures, Revised and Enlarged Edition, *Gottfried Haberler*—1961

The Patchwork History of Foreign Aid, *Lorna Morley* and *Felix Morley*—1961

U. S. Immigration Policy and World Population Problems, *Virgil Salera*—1960

*Inflation: Its Causes and Cures, *Gottfried Haberler*—1960

Voluntary Health Insurance in the United States, *Rita R. Campbell* and *W. Glenn Campbell*—1960

Unionism Reappraised: From Classical Unionism to Union Establishment, *Goetz Briefs*—1960

United States Aid and Indian Economic Development, *P. T. Bauer*—1959

Improving National Transportation Policy, *John H. Frederick*—1959

The Question of Governmental Oil Import Restrictions, *William H. Peterson*—1959

Labor Unions and the Concept of Public Service, *Roscoe Pound*—1959

Labor Unions and Public Policy, *Edward H. Chamberlain, Philip D. Bradley, Gerard D. Reilly*, and *Roscoe Pound*—1958. 177 pp. ($4.50)

National Aid to Higher Education, *George C. S. Benson* and *John M. Payne*—1958

Agricultural Surpluses and Export Policy, *Raymond F. Mikesell*—1958

The Economic Analysis of Labor Union power, *Edward H. Chamberlin*—1958

Post-War West German and United Kingdom Recovery, *David McCord Wright*—1957

The Regulation of Natural Gas, *James W. McKie*—1957

Legal Immunities of Labor Unions, *Roscoe Pound*—1957

*Automation—Its Impact on Economic Growth and Stability, *Almarin Phillips*—1957

*Involuntary Participation In Unionism, *Philip D. Bradley*—1956

The Role of Government in Developing Peaceful Uses of Atomic Energy, *Arthur Kemp*—1956

The Role of The Federal Government in Housing, *Paul F. Wendt*—1956

The Upper Colorado Reclamation Project, Pro by *Sen. Arthur V. Watkins*, Con by *Raymond Moley*—1956

*Federal Aid to Education—Boon or Bane? *Roger A. Freeman*—1955

States Rights and the Law of Labor Relations, *Gerard D. Reilly*—1955

Three Taft-Hartley Issues: Secondary Boycotts, "Mandatory" Injunctions, Replaced Strikers' Votes, *Theodore R. Iseman*—1955

What Price Federal Reclamation? *Raymond Moley*—1955

---

* Out of Print.

Private Investments Abroad, *Charles R. Carroll*—1954

Farm Price Supports—Rigid or Flexible, *Karl Brandt*—1954

*Currency Convertibility, *Gottfried Haberler*—1954

The Control of the Location of Industry in Great Britain, *John Jewkes*—1952

The Walsh-Healey Public Contracts Act, *John V. Van Sickle*—1952

The Economics of Full Employment: An Analysis of the U.N. Report on National and International Measures for Full Employment, *Wilhelm Röpke*—1952

Price Fixing for Foodstuffs, *Earl L. Butz*—1951

Manpower Needs and the Labor Supply, *Clarence D. Long*—1951

An Economic Approach to Antitrust Problems, *Clare E. Griffin*—1951, ($1.00)

*Valley Authorities, *Raymond Moley*—1950

*Farm Price and Income Supports, *O. B. Jesness*—1950

*Monetary Policy and Economic Prosperity: Testimony of Dr. W. W. Steward (July 3-4, 1930) before the Macmillan Committee with introduction by *Donald B. Woodward*—1950

Corporate Profits in Perspective, *John Linter*—1949

*Current Problems of Immigration Policy, *E. P. Hutchinson*—1949

Guaranteed Employment and Wage Plans. A Summary and Critique of the Latimer Report and Related Documents, *William A. Berridge* and *Cedric Wolfe*—1948

The Foreign Loan Policy of the United States, *J. B. Condliffe*—1947

*Proposals for Consideration by an International Conference on Trade and Employment, *J. B. Condliffe*—1946

The Market for Risk Capital, *Jules I. Bogen*—1946

For Studies 1953 and Earlier, Each Study 50 Cents Unless Otherwise Shown in Listing.

For all Studies 1954, to Date, Each Study One Dollar.

—————

* Out of Print.

LEGISLATIVE AND SPECIAL ANALYSES
87th Congress, First Session, 1961

No. 1—The Economic Status of the Aged. *A Special Analysis*

No. 2—Proposals for Federal Aid to Depressed Areas. Bills by *Sens. Douglas, et al., Dirksen, et al., Scott; Reps. Flood, Gray, Van Zandt, Morgan,* and *Saylor*

No. 3—Proposals to Provide Temporary Extended Unemployment Compensation Benefits. Bill by *Rep. Mills*

No. 4—Proposals to Amend the Fair Labor Standards Act of 1938. Bills by *Sens. Dirksen* and *McNamara; Rep. Roosevelt*

No. 5—Proposals for Federal Assistance in Financing Elementary and Second-ary Schools. Bills by *Sens. McNamara* and *Hart, Cooper, et al., Morse, et al.,* and others

No. 6—Proposed Social Security Amendments of 1961 (not including proposed health care benefits for the aged)

No. 7—Proposed Housing Act of 1961

No. 8—Proposals to Provide Health Care for the Aged Under Social Security. Bills by *Sens. McNamara, Anderson, Javits; Reps Gilbert, St. Germain, King*

No. 9—Proposals to Revise the Procedure for the Election of President and Vice President

No. 10—Proposals for Taxation of Foreign Source Income.

No. 11—Proposals to Prohibit Manufacturers of Motor Vehicles from Engaging in the Finance or Insurance Business: Bills by *Sen. Kefauver; Rep. Celler*

No. 12—The "Truth in Lending" Bill. Bill by *Sen. Douglas, et al.*

No. 13—The Drug Bill. Bill by *Sens. Kefauver* and *Hart*

No. 14—The Berlin Crisis: Part I: Background. *A Special Analysis*

No. 15—The Berlin Crisis: Part II: Elements of U. S. National Strategy. *A Special Analysis*

No. 16—The Berlin Crisis: Part III: Legal and Economic Factors, Proposals, and Strategic Lines of Action. *A Special Analysis*

87th Congress, Second Session, 1962

No. 1—The Proposal to Increase the National Debt Ceiling

No. 2—Reorganization Plan No. 1, of 1962 to Create a Department of Urban Affairs and Housing

No. 3—Foreign Trade: Part I: The Operation, Administration, and Development of the Trade Agreements Program. *A Special Analysis*

No. 4—Foreign Trade: Part II: Economic Consequences of Trade Liberalization. *A Special Analysis*

No. 5—Foreign Trade: Part III: Import Adjustment Assistance and Alternatives. *A Special Analysis*

No. 6—Foreign Trade: Part IV: The European Economic Community (Common Market). *A Special Analysis*

No. 7—Purchase of United Nations Bonds. Bill by *Sen. Sparkman*

No. 8—Foreign Trade: Part V: Proposals to Amend and Extend the Reciprocal Trade Agreements Legislation. *A Special Analysis*

No. 9—Proposals to Provide Health Care for the Aged Under Social Security. Bills by *Sen. Anderson, et al.; Rep. King*

No. 10—Tax Proposals Relating to Foreign Income. Bill by *Rep. Mills*

No. 11—Public Welfare Amendments of 1962. Bill by *Rep. Mills*

No. 12—The Drug Control Bills and Other Proposals to Amend the Food, Drug and Cosmetic Act. Bills by *Sen. Kefauver; Reps. Sullivan, Celler* and *Harris*

No. 13—The Proposed International Coffee Agreement. *A Special Analysis*

No. 14—The Pacific Northwest Power Preference Bills. Bills by *Sen. Anderson; Reps. Hansen* and *Pfost*

88th Congress, First Session, 1963

No. 1—History and Powers of the House Committee on Rules. *A Special Analysis*

Single Copy One Dollar

69